*Manhaj al-Sālikīn wa Tawḍīḥ al Fiqh fī al Dīn*

# The Path of the Wayfarer and the Clarification of *Fiqh* of The Religion

*Manhaj al-Sālikīn wa Tawḍīḥ al Fiqh fī al Dīn*
*By Sheikh ʿAbd al Raḥmān al Saʿdī*

## Vol.II

## The Fiqh of Social Dealings

Translated by Alomgir Ali
Tawfīq Online Learning

ISBN: 9798587619685

# Table of Contents

# TRANSLATOR'S INTRODUCTION FOR VOL.II

*Alḥamdulillāh*, by the grace of Allāh ﷻ, the final volume of *Manhaj al Sālikīn* has now been published approximately one-and-a-half years after publishing Volume I. This project began many years ago in 2006 and was almost abandoned on a number of occasions. As my first major attempt of translating a text in *fiqh*, it suffered from numerous problems and thus had to be revised many times. It may never be perfect, as the human eye is prone to overlooking mistakes, however one hopes that it is an accurate rendition of the original Arabic text and that it sufficiently conveys the intent of the author.

Translating the section on social dealings is generally considered to be more difficult than the section on worship. Hence, you will often find many incomplete translations of *fiqh* manuals. We therefore hope that this humble publication will help fill that void. It should however be noted that after the publication of Volume I of *Manhaj al Sālikīn*, the second volume of Dr Hatem al-Haj's – *waffaqahullāh* – translation of *ʿUmdah al Fiqh* by Ibn Qudāmah was published.[1]

Due to the nature of traditional *fiqh* manuals, navigating oneself through them will be a very difficult task. It is strongly advised that one reads this text with a teacher, as it

---

[1] Published by IIPH

is very easy to misunderstand terse *fiqh* manuals.[2] In the introduction to Volume I, I listed noteworthy translations of Ḥanbalī *fiqh* manuals. Since then, two more valuable translations have also been published:

1. "The Student's Guide" – a translation of the section of worship from *Dalīl al Ṭālib* by al Karmī, translated by my good friend, Jewel Jalil. (Published by Dar al-Arqam, UK)
2. The section of worship from *ʿUmdah al Ṭālib* by al Bahūtī, translated by John Starling. (Published by hanbalidisciples.com)

Finally, I would like to thank Dr. Salah Sharief[3] for doing an excellent job in proofreading the translation.

May Allāh ﷻ accept this humble effort, grant Paradise to its author, and forgive its translator.

Alomgir Ali
Tawfīq Online Learning
London
12th Jumāda al Ākhirah, 1442
24/1/21

[2] The section on worship has been taught twice on Tawfīq Online, and this volume has been taught once online as well. We aim to offer a pre-recorded course that covers the content of this volume in the near future *inshāʾAllāh*. Tawfīq Online Learning currently offers pre-recorded classes for vol.I of this book on its website. Visit www.tawfiqonline.org for more information.

[3] www.wordsmiths.org.uk

## TRANSLATOR'S INTRODUCTION FOR VOL.I

Studying *fiqh* is a duty upon every believer to ensure that their worship is sound and correct according to the dictates of Islamic teachings. Often, we find ourselves in situations where we do not know whether certain acts have invalidated our acts of worship, or whether certain aspects of our worship are recommended or obligatory. People then often share these concerns with others only to be confounded by a barrage of different views and opinions. Learning *fiqh* in an organised and structured manner allows a person to deal with such predicaments. It should therefore be of no surprise that having a deeper understanding of the Religion is from the signs that Allāh ﷻ wishes good for a person. Hence, the Prophet ﷺ said, "If Allāh ﷻ wishes good for someone, he grants him *fiqh* (i.e. a sound understanding) of the religion."[4] When explaining this *ḥadīth*, Ibn Ḥajar ﷺ mentioned the following, "The implied meaning of this *ḥadīth* is that the one who does not learn the *fiqh* of the religion – the governing principles of *Islām* as well as the subsidiary matters associated with those principles – has been denied goodness. Abū Yaʿlā ﷺ narrated another weak version of the *ḥadīth* of

---

[4] Bukhārī

Mu'āwiyah ﷺ with the additional sentence, "Allāh ﷻ has no concern for the one who does not learn the *fiqh* of the religion." Though weak, its meaning is sound, since the one who does not learn the affairs of his religion and is not a scholar of *fiqh*, nor a student of it, can be correctly described as being someone who good was not intended for."[5]

*Manhaj al Sālikīn* is a basic text that introduces the topic of *fiqh* for the layperson. It certainly does not answer all of one's *fiqh* related questions. Nevertheless, it is a good place to start. It is a text I began translating well over a decade ago as well as being my first major translation project, and so it suffered from many shortcomings, errors, and typos, as one would expect. I have since revised the translation and have had it checked by numerous friends and colleagues to try and sift out all of the errors. I also take the opportunity to declare that all previous versions of this translation that were handed to other teachers and students are now obsolete and should not be used.

It should be further noted that although the text is primarily based upon the (School) of Imām Aḥmad ﷺ,[6] the author, on a number of occasions, has chosen to depart from the *mathhab* in favour of what he believes to be more correct.

_____

[5] *Fatḥ al Bārī* 1/165

[6] Sheikh al-Saʿdī wrote to his student Sheikh Ibn ʿAqīl the following, "We have summarised it (i.e. *Manhaj al Sālikīn*) to the extent that it has become shorter than the *Mukhtaṣar* of *Al Muqniʿ* (i.e. *Zād al Mustaqniʿ*), *Akhṣar al Mukhtaṣarāt,* and *al ʿUmdah...*" All these texts are standard Ḥanbalī texts. See *al Ajwibah al Nāfiʿah* p.97-98.

This can make it somewhat difficult for the student of the *mathhab* to deal with. For that reason, I personally believe that this text is more suited for the absolute layman who does not intend to formally study *fiqh* beyond this text. In such a case, I believe this text does a good job of teaching the basic and required information that every layperson ought to know. As for the more avid seeker of knowledge, one way to deal with this predicament is by referring to a ḥanbalised version of the text, which was recently published by Sheikh Muḥammad ʿAbdul Wāḥid al Ḥanbalī al Azharī, *"Taḥqīq al Raghābāt bi Ḥanbalah Manhaj al Ṣālikīn wa Ziyādāt."*[7] Otherwise, it is perhaps best to refer to other available texts in *ḥanabli fiqh* that have been published in English, such as:

- "An Epitome of Ḥanbalī Substantive Law." By Yūsuf ibn ʿAbd al Hādī al Ḥanbalī, *Dar al Arqam*, 2018.
- "Hanbali Acts of Worship." From Ibn Balbān's *The Supreme Synopnis (Akhṣar al Mukhtaṣarāt)*, *Islamosaic*, 2016.
- "Supplement for The Seeker of Certitude" Worship from *Zād al Mustaqniʿ* by al Ḥajjāwī, *Islamosaic*, 2016.
- "Qaddūmī's Elementary Ḥanbalī Primer" a translation of *"al Ajwibah al Jaliyyah fi al Aḥkām al Ḥanbaliyyah."* 2013.
- *"Bidāyat al ʿĀbid"* By al Baʿlī, *Two Palm Press*, 2016.
- *"Fiqh of Worship"* (from *ʿUmdah al Fiqh* by Ibn Qudāmah), *IIPH*, 2011.

---

[7] Published by *Dār al Nūr al Mubīn*, Amman, Jordan. 2019

## Translation of the text

I have relied on the *Dār Ibn al Jawzī* (KSA) edition, 1st print (1424h/2003). Please note that the numbering system of the text was added by the editor, Muḥammad al Khuḍayrī, and not by Sheikh al Saʿdī himself. Nonetheless, it was decided to keep the numbering system, as it will help to break-down and study the *masāʾil* of the text. The translation only covers the section of worship. However, a second volume will be published in the near future - *inshāʾAllāh* - covering the remaining chapters of the book.

Finally, I would like to thank all of those who helped in preparing this publication, in particular Abdus Samad Ahmed, Shaheed Uddin, and everyone else who helped with the proofreading of the text.

A special mention of my wife, Umm Hanifah, must be mentioned. Despite the many hours I spend at my desk on a daily basis, she has always been supportive of my work and considerate enough to work around my commitments. May Allāh ﷻ accept this effort and make it a means for people to learn and practice their faith. *Āmīn.*

Alomgir Ali
London
1ˢᵗ of *Ramaḍān* 1440, 6ᵗʰ of May 2019
Tawfīq Online Learning

# كِتَابُ الْبُيُوع

# The Book of Transactions
### (Conditions of transactions)

**311.** The general ruling concerning transactions is that they are permissible. Allāh ﷻ says:

*"Allāh has permitted trade and forbidden usury."* (2: 275)

**312.** Thus, all commodities, including property, animals, furniture, and so on are permissible to place in contracts for sale if the conditions for selling are met.

**313.** The most important conditions are:

1. **(1ˢᵗ condition)** *Riḍā* (mutual consent), as per the saying of Allāh ﷻ:

   *"O You who believe, do not wrongfully consume each other's wealth, but [rather] trade by mutual consent. (4:29)*

**314. (2ⁿᵈ condition)** That there is no *gharar* (risk) nor *jahālah* (something that is not definitively known), since the Prophet *"forbade the transaction which involves risk (or uncertainty)."* (Muslim)

# كِتَابُ البُيُوعِ
## شُرُوطُ البَيْعِ

٣١١. الأَصْلُ فِيهِ الحِلُّ، قَالَ تَعَالَى: ﴿وَأَحَلَّ اللَّهُ البَيْعَ وَحَرَّمَ الرِّبَا﴾ [البقرة: ٢٧٥]

٣١٢. فَجَمِيعُ الأَعْيَانِ مِنْ عَقَارٍ وَحَيَوَانٍ وَأَثَاثٍ وَغَيْرِهَا – يَجُوزُ إِيقَاعُ العُقُودِ عَلَيْهَا إِذَا تَمَّتْ شُرُوطُ البَيْعِ.

٣١٣. فَمِنْ أَعْظَمِ الشُّرُوطِ: (الشَّرْطُ الأَوَّلُ): الرِّضَا، لِقَوْلِهِ تَعَالَى: ﴿إِلَّا أَنْ تَكُونَ تِجَارَةً عَنْ تَرَاضٍ مِنْكُمْ﴾

[النِّسَاء: ٢٩]

٣١٤. (الشَّرْطُ الثَّانِي): وَأَنْ لَا يَكُونَ فِيهَا غَرَرٌ وَجَهَالَةٌ؛ لِأَنَّ النَّبِيَّ ﷺ «نَهَى عَنْ بَيْعِ الغَرَرِ». رَوَاهُ مُسْلِمٌ

**315.** The following examples are included in such types of [forbidden] transactions:

1.  The selling of an *ābiq* (runaway slave) and a *shārid* (runaway camel).
2.  If one were to say, "I will sell to you one of the following two items."
3.  Selling an area of land determined by a stone's throw.
4.  Selling the unborn child of a slave, or to sell the fruit of a tree before it has grown.
5.  Selling the unborn offspring of an animal.

All of this applies to the above, whether the ambiguity involved was in the price of the item or the commodity itself.

**316. (3rd condition)** The contracting party must own the asset or have permission to deal with it, be mature, and competent in financial matters.

**317. (4<sup>th</sup> condition)** There should be no *ribā* (interest) in the transaction.

٣١٥. فَيَدْخُلُ فِيهِ:

١. بَيْعُ الآبِقِ وَالشَّارِدِ.

٢. وَأَنْ يَقُولَ بِعْتُكَ إِحْدَى السِّلْعَتَيْنِ.

٣. أَوْ بِمِقْدَارِ مَا تَبْلُغُ الحَصَاةُ مِنَ الأَرْضِ وَنَحْوِهِ.

٤. أَوْ مَا تَحْمِلُ أَمَتُهُ أَوْ شَجَرَتُهُ.

٥. أَوْ مَا فِي بَطْنِ الحَامِلِ.

وَسَوَاءٌ كَانَ الغَرَرُ فِي الثَّمَنِ أَوِ المُثَمَّنِ.

٣١٦. (الشَّرْطُ الثَّالِثُ):

وَأَنْ يَكُونَ العَاقِدُ مَالِكًا لِلشَّيْءِ، أَوْ مَأْذُونًا لَهُ فِيهِ وَهُوَ بَالِغٌ رَشِيدٌ.

٣١٧. وَمِنْ شُرُوطِ البَيْعِ أَيْضًا: أَنْ لَا يَكُونَ فِيهِ رِبًا

On the authority of ʿUbādah ﷺ the Prophet ﷺ said, "Gold is to be paid for by gold, silver by silver, wheat by wheat, barley by barley, dates by dates, and salt by salt; like for like and equal for equal. If these classes differ, then sell as you wish if payment is made hand to hand. Whoever gives more or asks for more has engaged in *ribā*." (Muslim)

**318.** Thus, it is not permissible to exchange an item that is customarily sold by volume – from one of these categories – with another item of the same kind, unless these two conditions have been met. This also applies to goods that are customarily sold by weight.

**319.** The exchange of an item customarily sold by volume, for another of a different kind, or the exchange of an item that is customarily sold by weight, for another of a different kind, is permissible as long as the exchange is simultaneous (*taqābuḍ*) and before the buyer and seller part company.

**320.** It is permissible for an item customarily sold by volume to be exchanged for one customarily sold by weight, or vice versa, even if the exchange takes place after they part company.

**321.** Being unaware of *tamāthul* (equivalence of two amounts) is equivalent to being certain of *tafāḍul* (where two amounts differ).

عَنْ عُبَادَةَ رَضِيَّ اللهُ عَنْهُ قَالَ: قَالَ رَسُولُ اللهِ ﷺ «الذَّهَبُ بِالذَّهَبِ، وَالْفِضَّةُ بِالْفِضَّةِ، وَالْبُرُّ بِالْبُرِّ، وَالشَّعِيرُ بِالشَّعِيرِ، وَالتَّمْرُ بِالتَّمْرِ، وَالْمِلْحُ بِالْمِلْحِ، مِثْلاً بِمِثْلٍ سَوَاءً بِسَوَاءٍ، فَإِذَا اخْتَلَفَتْ هَذِهِ الأَصْنَافُ فَبِيعُوا كَيْفَ شِئْتُمْ، إِذَا كَانَ يَدًا بِيَدٍ، فَمَنْ زَادَ أَوْ اسْتَزَادَ فَقَدْ أَرْبَى» رَوَاهُ مُسْلِمٌ.

٣١٨. فَلَا يُبَاعُ مَكِيلٌ بِمَكِيلٍ مِنْ جِنْسِهِ إِلَّا بِهَذَيْنِ الشَّرْطَيْنِ، وَلَا مَوْزُونٌ بِجِنْسِهِ إِلَّا كَذَلِكَ.

٣١٩. وَإِنْ بِيعَ مَكِيلٌ بِمَكِيلٍ مِنْ غَيْرِ جِنْسِهِ، أَوْ مَوْزُونٌ بِمَوْزُونٍ مِنْ غَيْرِ جِنْسِهِ: جَازَ بِشَرْطِ التَّقَابُضِ قَبْلَ التَّفَرُّقِ.

٣٢٠. وَإِنْ بِيعَ مَكِيلٌ بِمَوْزُونٍ أَوْ عَكْسِه جَازَ وَلَوْ كَانَ القَبْضُ بَعْدَ التَّفَرُّقِ

٣٢١. وَالجَهْلُ بِالتَّمَاثُلِ كَالعِلْمِ بِالتَّفَاضُلِ

**322.** The Prophet ﷺ likewise prohibited *muzābanah*, which is the "selling fresh dates still on trees for dried dates." (Agreed upon)

**323.** "The Prophet ﷺ gave concession for *'arāyā* (selling unpicked dates) by their estimated weight when dried. This is on condition that they are less than five *awsuq*[8] to the one in need of fresh dates (*ruṭab*) if the person does not have enough money to buy them." (Muslim).

**324. (5ᵗʰ condition):** That the item for sale is not forbidden according to the Islamic law:

- Either due to the essence of the item itself, like intoxicants, carrion, and idols, which were all forbidden by the Prophet ﷺ. (Agreed upon)
- Or due to the sale resulting in the breaking of ties with a Muslim or causing animosity between two Muslims. Thus, the Prophet ﷺ forbade "undercutting someone in a sale, offering to pay more than someone in a given trade, and bidding up the price of some merchandise that one is not interested in (*najash*)." (Agreed upon)
- Likewise, the Prophet ﷺ forbade the separation of slaves who are family members.

---

[8] Pl. of *wasq*, which is equivalent to a camel load (approx 60 ṣā' or 165 litres).

٣٢٢. كَمَا نَهَى النَّبِيُّ ﷺ عَنْ بَيْعِ المُزَابَنَةِ: «وَهُوَ شِرَاءُ التَّمر بِالتَّمرِ فِي رُؤُوسِ النَّخْلِ» مُتَّفَقٌ عَلَيْهِ

٣٢٣. «وَرَخَّصَ فِي بَيْعِ العَرَايَا، بِخَرْصِهَا، فِيمَا دُونَ خَمْسَةِ أَوْسُقٍ، لِلْمُحْتَاجِ إِلَى الرُّطَبِ، وَلَا ثَمَنَ عِنْدَهُ يَشْتَرِي بِهِ، بِخَرْصِهَا» رَوَاهُ مُسْلِمٌ

(الشَّرْطُ الخَامِسُ):

٣٢٤. وَمِنَ الشُّرُوطِ: أَنْ لَا يَقَعَ العَقْدُ عَلَى مُحَرَّمٍ شَرْعًا:

- إِمَّا لِعَيْنِهِ، كَمَا نَهَى النَّبِيُّ ﷺ «عَنْ بَيْعِ الخَمْرِ وَالْمَيْتَةِ وَالْأَصْنَامِ.» مُتَّفَقٌ عَلَيْهِ.

- وَإِمَّا لِمَا يَتَرَتَّبُ عَلَيْهِ مِنْ قَطِيعَةِ المُسْلِمِ، كَمَا نَهَى النَّبِيُّ ﷺ «عَنِ البَيْعِ عَلَى بَيْعِ المُسْلِمِ، وَالشِّرَاءِ عَلَى شِرَائِهِ، وَالنَّجْشِ» متفق عليه

- وَمِن ذَلِكَ نَهْيُهُ ﷺ عَنِ التَّفْرِيقِ بَيْنَ ذِي الرَّحِمِ فِي الرَّقِيقِ

- Likewise, a transaction where it is known that the buyer will perform a sin with the item he buys, such as walnuts and eggs for gambling or weapons to create *fitnah* (civil strife) or for highway robbers.
- The Prophet ﷺ also forbade going to meet merchants before they reach the marketplace for sale. He ﷺ said, "Do not meet the merchant on the way to the market and enter into a business transaction with him. Whoever meets him and buys from him and then the owner [of the merchandise] comes into the market [and finds that he has been paid a lower price], he has the option [to declare the transaction null and void]." (Muslim).
- The Prophet ﷺ also said, "Whoever cheats us is not from us". (Muslim).

**325.** An example of clear usury is:

1. Using a loophole by the way of *ʿīnah,* which is to sell a commodity on credit then buy the commodity from the buyer in cash for less, or the opposite.
2. Subterfuge by way of issuing another loan.
3. Using a loophole by lending someone money stipulating that the lender receives some sort of benefit from something the debtor owns, or for him to be paid in the form of a benefit. This is because every loan that leads to a type of benefit is considered usury.

- ومِنْ ذَلِكَ: إِذَا كَانَ المُشْتَرِي تَعْلَم مِنهُ أَنَّهُ يَفْعَلُ المَعْصِيَةَ بِما اِشْتَراهُ، كَاشْتِراءِ الجَوْزِ والبَيْضِ لِلْقِمارِ، أَوْ السِّلاحِ لِلْفِتْنَةِ، وعَلى قُطَّاعِ الطُّرُقِ،

- وَنَهْيُهُ ﷺ عَنْ تَلَقِّي الجَلَبِ، فَقالَ: «لا تَلَقَّوْا الجَلَبَ، فَمَن تَلَقَّى فاشترى منه، فإذا أتى سيده السوق، فهو بالخيار» رواه مسلم

- وقالَ ﷺ «مَن غَشَّنا فَلَيْسَ مِنّا». رَواهُ مُسْلِمٌ.


٣٢٥. ومِثْلُ الرّبا الصَّريحِ:

١. التَّحَيُّل عَلَيْهِ بِالعِينَةِ، بِأَنْ يَبِيعَ سِلْعَةً بِمِائَةٍ إِلى أَجَلٍ، ثُمَّ يَشْتَرِيها مِن مُشْتَرِيها بِأَقَلَّ مِنها نَقْدًا، أَوْ بالعكس.

٢. أَوْ التَّحَيُّلُ عَلى قَلْبِ الدَّينِ.

٣. أَوْ التَّحَيُّلُ عَلى الرّبا بِقَرْضٍ، بِأَنْ يُقْرِضَهُ ويَشْتَرِطَ الاِنْتِفاعَ بِشَيْءٍ مِن مالِهِ، أَوْ إِعْطاءَهُ عَنْ ذَلِكَ عِوَضًا، فَكُلُّ قَرْضٍ جَرَّ نَفْعًا فَهُوَ رِبًا.

4. Likewise, to exchange silver jewellery along with something else for silver, or a handful of ʿajwah dates and a *dirham* for two *dirhams.*

**326.** The Prophet ﷺ was once asked about selling dry dates (*tamr*) for fresh dates (*ruṭab*). He ﷺ replied, "Do they decrease [in volume] when they dry?" They said yes, so the Prophet ﷺ prohibited such a type of transaction. (Reported by Abū Dāwūd and others)

**327.** The Prophet ﷺ also forbade the selling of a pile of dates of an unknown quantity for dates which had a known quantity. (Muslim)

**328.** It is permissible to sell something one that one is owed, only to a person who owes it, on the condition that the one who is owed takes possession of the replacement item before they part company, and that there is nothing left between them. This is as per the statement of the Prophet ﷺ, "There is nothing wrong if you take [the equivalent] as long as it is done according to the rate of the day, and you part with nothing left between you." However, if it is sold to someone else, the transaction is invalid because it would involve *gharar* (risk/uncertainty).

٤. وَمِن التَّحَيُّلِ: بَيْعُ حُلِيِّ فِضَّةٍ مَعَهُ غَيْرُهُ بِفِضَّةٍ، أَوْ مُدّ عَجْوَةٍ ودرهم بدرهم.

٣٢٦. وسُئِل النبي ﷺ عن بيع التَّمْرِ بِالرُّطَبِ، فقَالَ: «أَيَنْقُصُ إذا جَفَّ؟» قالُوا: نعم، فنهى عن ذلك. رواه الخمسة

٣٢٧. وَنَهى عَنْ بَيْعِ الصبرة مِنَ التَّمْرِ لا يُعْلَم مَكِيلها، بالكيل المسَمَّى بالتَّمر. رَواهُ مُسْلِمٌ

٣٢٨. وأمَّا بَيْعُ ما فِي الذِّمَّةِ فإنْ كانَ عَلى مَن هُوَ عَلَيْهِ جازَ، وذلِكَ بِشَرْطِ قَبْضِ عِوَضِهِ قَبْلَ التَّفَرُّقِ؛ لِقَوْلِهِ ﷺ: «لا بَأْسَ أَنْ تَأْخُذَها بِسِعْرِ يَوْمِها، ما لَمْ تَتَفَرَّقا، وبَيْنَكُما شَيْءٌ» رَواهُ الخَمْسَةُ. وإنْ كانَ على غيره لا يصح؛ لأنه غرر.

بَاب بَيْعِ الأُصُولِ والثِّمَار

# Selling Immovables and Produce

**329.** The Prophet ﷺ said, "Whoever sells a palm tree after it has been pollinated will keep the fruits unless the buyer stipulates them [for himself]." (Agreed upon)

**330.** This also applies to all other trees if their fruits are apparent and visible.

**331.** This also applies to crops that appear which are usually harvested only once a year.

**332.** If, however, the crops are usually harvested many times, then the plants will belong to the buyer, and the fruits at the time of the sale will belong to the seller.

**333.** The Prophet ﷺ forbade the sale of fruits until the condition of the fruits is known. He forbade it for the buyer and seller. (Agreed upon)

**334.** The Prophet ﷺ was asked about the phrase "until the condition of the fruits is known" to which he replied, "until they were safe from blight." And in another narration, "Until they become reddish or yellowish."

# بابُ بَيعِ الأُصُولِ والثِّمارِ

**٣٢٩.** قــالَ ﷺ: «مَنْ بَــاعَ نَخْلًا بَعْــدَ أَنْ تُؤَبَّر فثمرتها للبائع، إلا أن يشترطها المبتاع» متفق عليه

**٣٣٠.** وكذَلِكَ سائِرُ الأشجارِ إذاكانَ ثمَرُهُ بادِيًا.

**٣٣١.** ومِثْلُهُ إذا ظَهَرَ الزَّرعُ الذِي لا يُحْصَدُ إلّا مَرَّةً واحِدَةً.

**٣٣٢.** فإنْ كانَ يُحْصَدُ مِرارًا فالأُصُولُ لِلْمُشتَرِي، والجَزَّةُ الظّاهِرةُ عِنْدَ البَيعِ لِلبائِعِ.

**٣٣٣.** وهى رسولُ الله ﷺ عن بَيعِ الثِّمارِ حَتَّى يَبْدُوَ صَلاحُها: نَهى البائِعَ والمُبتاعَ.

**٣٣٤.** وسُئِلَ عَنْ صَلاحِها، فَقالَ: «حَتَّى تَذْهَبَ عاهَتُهُ»، وفِي لَفْظِ: «حَتَّى تَحْمارَّ أو تَصْفارَّ»

**335.** He ﷺ also forbade selling grain until they have hardened. (Abū Dāwūd and others)

**336.** He ﷺ also said, "If you sell fruit to your brother and it was affected by blight, it is not permissible for you to take anything from him. How could you take your brother's wealth unjustly?" (Reported by Muslim)

٣٣٥. وَنَهَى عَنْ بَيْعِ الحَبِّ حَتَّى يَشْتَدَّ. رَوَاهُ أَهْلُ السنن.

٣٣٦. وقال: «لَوْ بِعْتَ مِنْ أَخِيكَ ثَمَرًا فَأَصَابَتْهُ جَائِحَةٌ فَلَا يَحِلُّ لَكَ أَنْ تَأْخُذَ مِنْهُ شيئًا، بِمَ تَأْخُذُ مَالَ أَخِيكَ بِغَيْرِ حَقٍّ؟» رواه مسلم

# باب الخِيَار وغَيْره
# Chapter: The Option to Revoke a Deal (*Khiyār*)

337. Once a transaction concludes it becomes binding upon both parties except for a valid legal reason. From amongst the valid reasons are:

338. *Khiyār al Majlis:* (The option to revoke the deal during the contracting session). The Prophet ﷺ said, "When two men enter into a transaction, each of them has the choice [of annulling it] so long as they have not yet parted and are still together, or one of them has given the option or choice to the other. Once he has accepted the terms of the other, then the transaction is binding." (Agreed upon)

339. *Khiyār ash-Sharṭ:* (The option to revoke the deal based on a stipulation). This is where exercising the right to revoke is stipulated by both parties, or for one of the two for a certain fixed period.

The Prophet ﷺ said, "Muslims must abide by the conditions they make unless the condition makes the impermissible permissible, or the permissible impermissible." (Reported in the *Sunan*)

# بابُ الخيارِ وغيرِه

٣٣٧. وإذا وقَعَ العَقْدُ صارَ لازمًا، إلا بسبب من الأسباب الشرعية، فَمِنها:

٣٣٨. خِيارُ المَجلِسِ: قالَ النَّبيُّ ﷺ: «إذا تَبايَعَ الرَّجُلانِ فَكُلُّ واحِدٍ مِنهُما بالخِيارِ، ما لَمْ يَتَفَرَّقا وكانا جَميعًا، أوْ يُخَيِّرُ أَحَدُهُما الآخَرَ، فإنْ خَيَّرَ أَحَدُهُما الآخَرَ فَتَبايَعا ولَمْ يَتْرُكْ واحِدٌ مِنهُما البَيعَ، فَقَدْ وجَبَ البَيعُ» مُتَّفَقٌ عَلَيْهِ.

٣٣٩. ومِنها: خِيارُ الشَّرْطِ، إذا شَرَطَ الخِيارَ لَهُما أوْ لِأَحَدِهِما مدةً معلومة

قالَ النَّبيُّ ﷺ: «المسْلِمُونَ عِنْدَ شُرُوطِهِمْ، إلّا شَرْطًا أحلَّ حَرامًا أوْ حرَّم حَلالًا» رَواهُ أَهْلُ السُّنَنِ

**340.** If one were significantly duped either by *najash* (intentionally increasing the bidding price with no intent to purchase the item), or by going out to meet the merchant before they reached the marketplace, they have the right to revoke the deal.

**341.** *Khiyār al Tadlīs* (The option to revoke the deal in the case of fraud). This is where the seller cheats the buyer in order to raise the price of the commodity. An example of that would be leaving the milk in the udder of animals to accumulate. The Prophet ﷺ said, "Do not keep camels and sheep without milking them for a long time. Whoever buys such an animal has the option to milk it and then decide whether to keep it or return it to the owner with one ṣāʿ of dates." (Agreed upon) In another narration, it mentions that the buyer has the option of revoking the deal for up to three days.

**342.** If one purchases a product with a defect not knowing the problem with it at the time of purchase, then he has the option to either return the product or keep it. If, however, he was unable to return the product due to a specific reason, he has a right to compensation.

**343.** If both parties disagree over the price of the product then they are both to take an oath. Thereafter, they both have the right to revoke the deal.

٣٤٠. ومِنها: إذا غُبِنَ غِبْنًا يَخْرُجُ عَنِ العادَةِ، إمّا بِنَجشٍ، أَوْ تَلَقِّي الجَلَبَ أَوْ غَيْرِهِما.

٣٤١. ومِنها: خِيارُ التَّدْلِيسِ: بِأَنْ يُدَلِّسَ البائِعُ عَلى المشْتَرِي ما يَزِيدُ بِهِ الثَّمَنَ، كَتَصْرِيَةِ اللَّبَنِ في ضَرْعِ بهيمة الأنعام،

قالَ ﷺ: «لا تُصَرُّوا الإبِلَ والغَنَمَ، فَمَنِ ابْتاعَها بَعْدُ فَهُوَ بِخَيْرِ النَّظَرَيْنِ بَعْدَ أَنْ يَحْلُبَها، إنْ شاءَ أَمْسَكَها، وإنْ شاءَ رَدَّها، وصاعًا مِن تَمْرٍ» مُتَّفَقٌ عَلَيْهِ، وفي لَفْظٍ: «فَهُوَ بِالخِيارِ ثَلاثَةَ أيّامٍ».

٣٤٢. وإذا اشترى معيبًا لم يعلم عيبه فله الخيار بين ردّه وإمساكه، فإن تعذر رده تعين أرشه.

٣٤٣. وإذا اخْتَلَفا في الثَّمَنِ تَحالَفا، ولِكُلٍّ مِنهُما الفَسْخُ

**344.** The Prophet ﷺ said, "Whoever agrees with a Muslim to cancel a transaction, Allāh ﷻ will forgive his sins on the Day of Resurrection." (Reported by Abū Dāwūd and Ibn Mājah)

٣٤٤. وقالَ ﷺ: «مَن أقالَ مُسْلِمًا بَيْعَتِهِ أقالَهُ اللَّهُ عَثْرَتَهُ» رَواهُ أبو داود وابن ماجه

# بَاب السَلَم

# Chapter: Buying in Advance

345. Advance payment is permissible for everything that can be described with definite properties on condition that:

1. All characteristics that could vary the price are explicitly stated.
2. There is a specified time for receiving [the item]
3. The price of the item must be paid for entirely in advance before the two parties separate.

It was reported on the authority of Ibn ʿAbbās ؓ that when the Prophet ﷺ came to *Madīnah* he found the people paying in advance for fruits which were to be given after one, two, or even 3 years after. He ﷺ then said, "Whoever pays in advance should pay for a specified measurement and a specified weight for a specific period." (Agreed upon)

The Prophet ﷺ also said, "Whoever takes the wealth of people intending to repay it, Allāh ﷻ will pay it on his behalf, and whoever takes it in order to destroy it, then Allāh will destroy him." (Bukhārī)

# بابُ السَّلَمِ

٣٤٥. يَصِحُّ السَّلَمُ في كُلِّ ما يَنْضَبِطُ بِالصِّفَةِ:

١. إذا ضَبَطَهُ بِجَميعِ صِفاتِهِ التي يختلف بها الثمن.

٢. وذكر أجله.

٣. وأَعْطاه الثَّمَنَ قَبْلَ التَّفَرُّقِ

عن ابن عباس رضي الله عنهما قال: قدم النبي ﷺ المدينة وهم يُسْلِفُون في الثمار السنة والسنتين، فقال: «مَنْ أَسْلَفَ في شَيء فَلْيُسْلِفْ في كَيْلٍ مَعْلُومٍ، وَوَزْنٍ مَعْلُومٍ، إلى أَجَلٍ مَعْلُومٍ».

٣٤٦. وقال ﷺ: «مَن أَخَذَ أموالَ النَّاسِ يُريدُ أداءَها أَدّاها اللَّهُ عَنْهُ، ومَن أَخَذَها يُريدُ إتلافَها أَتْلَفَهُ اللَّهُ» رَواهُ البخاري

37

بَابُ الرَّهْن والضَّمَان والكَفَالَة

# Chapter: Collateral, Guaranteeing Payment & Appearance

**347.** These are methods of securing established financial rights.

**348.** It is valid to give a *rahn* (collateral) in the form of an *'ayn* (commodity) that is allowed to sell.

**349.** It will remain as an *amānah* (trust) with the *murtahin* (mortgagee) though he not liable for it unless he transgressed or was negligent, as is the case with all other trusts.

**350.** If complete redemption is achieved, the collateral should be released.

**351.** However, if full redemption is not achieved and the creditor seeks to sell the collateral, it is obligatory to sell it and use the money to pay back the creditor. Whatever remains from selling it belongs to the rightful owner. And anything that remains to be paid from the debt will remain a debt albeit unsecured.

**352.** Whoever damages the collateral has to compensate for it and that will become the collateral itself

# بابُ الرَّهْنِ والضَّمانِ والكَفالَةِ

٣٤٧. وهَذِهِ وثائِقُ بِالحُقُوقِ الثابتة.

٣٤٨. فالرهن، يَصِحُّ بِكُلِّ عَيْنٍ يَصِحُّ بَيْعُها.

٣٤٩. فَتَبْقى أمانَةٌ عِنْدَ المرْتَهِنِ، لا يَضْمَنُها، إِلَّا إنْ
تَعَدّى أوْ فَرَّطَ، كَسائِرِ الأماناتِ.

٣٥٠. فَإنْ حَصَلَ الوَفاءُ التّامُّ انْفَكَّ الرَّهْنُ.

٣٥١. وإنْ لَمْ يَحْصُلْ، وطَلَبَ صاحِبُ الحَقِّ بَيْعَ الرَّهْنِ
وجَبَ بَيْعُهُ والوَفاءُ مِن ثَمَنِهِ، وما بَقِيَ مِن الثَّمَنِ بَعْدَ وفاءِ
الحَقِّ فَلِرَبِّهِ، وإنْ بَقِيَ مِن الدَّيْنِ شَيْءٌ يَبْقى دَيْنًا مُرْسَلًا بِلا
رَهْنٍ.

٣٥٢. وإنْ أتْلَفَ الرَّهْنَ أحَدٌ فَعَلَيْهِ ضَمانُهُ يَكُونُ رَهْنًا

**353.** The growth of the collateral is considered to be a part of it, and the expenses for its maintenance are upon the owner.

**354.** It is not allowed for the one who gives the collateral (*rāhin*) to benefit from it without consent of the other party, or a provision given by Islamic law. The Prophet ﷺ said, "A riding animal can be ridden while it is mortgaged, and a milking animal can be milked while it is mortgaged, and it is upon the one riding and drinking [the milk] to maintain it." (Bukhārī)

**355.** *Ḍamān* is to guarantee the repayment of a debt by a third party.

**356.** *Kafālah* is to commit to present the debtor in person to the creditor.

**357.** The Prophet ﷺ said, "The guarantor is liable." (Abū Dāwūd)

**358.** Both are legally liable except if:

1.  He carries out what he is obliged to do, or
2.  The creditor acquits him, or
3.  The creditor acquits the original debtor.

And Allāh ﷻ knows best.

٣٥٣. وَنَمَاؤُهُ تَبَعٌ لَهُ، وَمُؤْنَتُهُ عَلَى رَبِّهِ.

٣٥٤. وَلَيْسَ لِلرَّاهِنِ الِانْتِفَاعُ بِهِ إِلَّا بِإِذْنِ الآخَرِ، أَوْ بِإِذْنِ الشَّارِعِ فِي قَوْلِهِ ﷺ: «الظَّهْرُ يُرْكَبُ بِنَفَقَتِهِ إِذَا كَانَ مَرْهُونًا، وَلَبَنُ الدَّرِّ يُشْرَبُ بِنَفَقَتِهِ إِذَا كَانَ مَرْهُونًا، وَعَلَى الَّذِي يَرْكَبُ وَيَشْرَبُ النَّفَقَةُ» رَوَاهُ البُخَارِيُّ.

٣٥٥. وَالضَّمَانُ: أَنْ يَضْمَنَ الحَقَّ عَنِ الَّذِي عَلَيْهِ.

٣٥٦. وَالكَفَالَةُ: أَنْ يَلْتَزِمَ بِإِحْضَارِ بَدَنِ الخَصْمِ.

٣٥٧. قَالَ ﷺ: «الزَّعِيمُ غَارِمٌ».

٣٥٨. فَكُلٌّ مِنْهُما ضَامِنٌ إِلَّا:

١. إِنْ قَامَ بِما الْتَزَمَ بِهِ،

٢. أَوْ أَبْرَأَهُ صَاحِبُ الحَقِّ،

٣. أَوْ بَرِئَ الأَصِيلُ.


وَاللهُ أَعْلَمُ.

# بَابُ الحَجرِ لِفَلَسٍ أَوْ غَيْرِهِ

# Chapter: Interdiction due to bankruptcy

**359.** A creditor should give respite to the one in financial difficulties (*muʿsir*).

**360.** He should also be easy on the one who is not facing such difficulties (*mūsir*).

**361.** Whoever is in debt must repay it completely in totality in amount and quality.

**362.** The Prophet ﷺ said, "Procrastination in paying debts by a wealthy man is injustice. So, if your debt is transferred from your debtor to a wealthy debtor, you should agree." (Agreed upon) This is considered to be a form of financial easing (*muyāsarah*)

**363.** The *malīʾ* is the one who is capable of paying back what is due and does not intentionally delay and can be brought to a court of law.

# بابُ الحَجرِ لِفَلَسٍ أوْ غيرِهِ

٣٥٩. ومَن لَهُ الحَقُّ فَعَلَيْهِ أَنْ يُنْظِرَ المُعْسِرَ.

٣٦٠. ويَنْبَغِي أَنْ يُيَسِّرَ عَلَى المُوْسِرِ.

٣٦١. ومَنْ عَلَيْهِ الحَقُّ فَعَلَيْهِ الوَفاءُ كامِلًا بِالقَدَرِ والصِّفَاتِ.

٣٦٢. قال ﷺ: «مَطْلُ الغَنِي ظُلْم، وَإذا أُحِيلَ بِدَيْنِهِ عَلَى مُلِيءٍ فَلْيَحْتَلْ» مُتَّفَقٌ عَلَيْهِ، وهَذا مِن المِياسَرَةِ.

٣٦٣. فالمَلِيءُ: هُوَ القادِرُ عَلَى الوَفاءِ، الذِي لَيْسَ مُماطِلًا، ويُمْكِنُ تَحْضِيرُهُ لِمَجْلِسِ الحُكْمِ.

**364.** If a person's debts amount to more than his wealth, and the creditors - or some of them - request a judge to interdict him, he should be interdicted. He should also be prevented from administrating his assets which should be liquidated then distributed amongst the creditors in accordance with the ratio of their debts.

**365.** None of the creditors should be given any preference over others except:

1. The one who has collateral in his possession.
2. The Prophet ﷺ said, "Whoever finds his wealth with an insolvent person, he will have more right to it than anybody else." (Agreed upon)

**366.** It is obligatory upon the guardian of the minor, incompetent, or insane to prevent them from administrating their wealth in a manner that will harm them.

Allāh ﷻ says, *"Do not hand over to the simple-minded any property of theirs for which Allah has made you responsible..."* (Al Nisāʾ: 5)

**367.** It is not allowed for them to control their wealth except if it is better than its retention, or if it leads to a beneficial outcome. Likewise, they will be allowed to approach it if they are in need of it.

٣٦٤. وإذا كانَتِ الدُّيُونُ أَكْثَرَ مِن مالِ الإِنْسانِ، وطَلَبِ الغُرَماءُ أَوْ بَعْضُهُمْ مِنَ الحاكِمِ أَنْ يَحْجِرَ عَلَيْهِ، حَجَرَ عَلَيْهِ، ومَنَعَهُ مِن التَّصَرُّفِ في جَمِيعِ مالِهِ، ثُمَّ يصفي ماله، ويُقَسِّمُهُ عَلى الغُرَماءِ بِقَدْرِ دُيُوهِمْ.

٣٦٥. ولا يُقَدِّمُ منهم إلا:

١. صاحِبَ الرَّهْنِ بِرَهْنِهِ.

٢. وقالَ ﷺ: «من أدرك ما له عِنْدَ رَجُلٍ قَدْ أَفْلَسَ فَهُوَ أَحَقُّ بِهِ من غيره» متفق عليه.

٣٦٦. ويجب على ولي الصغير والسفيه والمجنون، أن يمنعهم من التصرف في مالهم الذي يضرهم.

قال تعالى: ﴿ولا تُؤْتُوا السُّفَهاءَ أَمْوالَكُمُ الَّتِي جَعَلَ اللهُ لَكُمْ قِيامًا﴾ [النِّساء:٥]

٣٦٧. وعليه أَلا يقرب ما لهم إلَّا بِالتي هِيَ أَحْسَنُ مِن حفظِهِ، والتصرفِ النَّافِعِ لَهُمْ، وصرفِ ما يَحْتاجُونَ إِلَيْهِ مِنهُ.

**368.** Their guardian is their father who is responsible and competent in financial matters. If they do not have a father, the judge should appoint someone from their relatives who is most aware of their circumstances and is the most caring for them and is trustworthy.

**369.** If the guardian is rich, he should take no wages, but if he is poor, he may take for himself what is just and reasonable. This amount should be the minimum amount someone would charge for such a service.

And Allāh ﷻ knows best.

٣٦٨. ووَلِيُّهُمْ أَبُوهُمُ الرَّشِيدُ، فَإِنْ لَمْ يَكُنْ جَعَلَ الحاكِمُ الوَكالَةَ لأَشْفَقَ مَن يَجِدُهُ مِن أقارِبِهِ، وأعرفهم، وآمنهم.

٣٦٩. ومَن كانَ غَنِيًّا فَلْيَتَعَفَّفْ، ومَن كانَ فَقِيرًا فَلْيَأْكُلْ بِالمعْرُوفِ: وهُوَ الأَقَلُّ مِن أجرةِ مِثْلِهِ أو كفايته.

والله أعلم.

# بَابُ الصُّلْح

# Chapter: Conciliation

370. The Prophet ﷺ said, "Conciliation between Muslims is permissible, except for conciliation which makes the lawful unlawful and the unlawful lawful." (Abū Dāwūd and Tirmidhī)

371. It is permissible for the creditor to negotiate an agreement by the way of a corporeal item for another, or with a legal commitment.

372. It is permissible for the debtor to negotiate an agreement by offering a corporeal item in its place or by a legal commitment as long as the commitment is fulfilled before they part company.

373. It is also permissible to negotiate an agreement by allowing the creditor to benefit from his property or anything else as long as it is known. Moreover, it is permissible to settle a debt that is due in the future by repaying only part of it immediately. It is also permissible to negotiate an amount to settle a debt whose amount is unknown to both parties.

374. The Prophet ﷺ said, "None of you should refuse to let his neighbour fix a piece of wood to his wall." (Bukhārī)

# بابُ الصُّلْحِ

٣٧٠. قالَ النَّبيُّ ﷺ: «الصُّلْحُ جائزٌ بَيْنَ المسْلِمينَ، إلّا صُلْحًا حرَّم حلالًا أو أحل حرامًا». رَواهُ أبُو داوُدَ والتِّرْمِذيُّ. وقالَ: حَسَنٌ صَحِيحٌ، وصَحَّحَهُ الحاكِمُ

٣٧١. فإذا صالَحَهُ عَنْ عَيْنٍ بِعَيْنٍ أخرى، أبو بدَين: جازَ.

٣٧٢. وإنْ كانَ لَهُ عَلَيْهِ دَينٌ فصالَحَهُ عَنْهُ بِعَيْنٍ، أوْ بدَين قَبَضَهُ قَبْلَ التفرق: جاز.

٣٧٣. أوْ صالَحَهُ عَلى مَنفَعَةٍ في عَقارِهِ أوْ غَيْرِهِ مَعْلُومَةٍ، أوْ صالَحَ عَنِ الدَّيْنِ المؤَجَّلِ بِبَعْضِهِ حالًّا، أوْ كانَ لَهُ عَلَيْهِ دَيْنٌ لا يَعْلَمانِ قَدْرَهُ فصالَحَهُ عَلى شيْءٍ: صَحَّ ذلك

٣٧٤. وقالَ ﷺ: «لا يَمْنَعَنَّ جارٌ جارَهُ أنْ يَغْرِزَ خَشَبَهُ عَلى جِدارِهِ» رواه البخاري

# بَابُ الوَكَالَة والشَّرِكَة والمساقَاة والمزَارَعَة

# Chapter: Agency, Partnership & Crop Sharing

## (Agency)

375. The Prophet ﷺ used to appoint agents to deal with his private dealings and likewise public affairs that were related to him.

376. It is a non-binding form of contract from both parties.

377. It is valid for all matters in which representation is allowed including:

1. The rights of Allāh ﷻ, such as the distribution of *zakāh*, expiations, and so on.
2. The rights of other people, such as contracts and the termination of them, and so on.

378. Appointing an agent is not permitted for matters in which representation is not allowed, such as matters that are specifically connected to a particular individual, like prayer, purification, oaths, dividing time among one's wives, and so on.

# بابُ الوَكالَةِ والشَّرِكَةِ والمُساقاةِ والمُزارَعَةِ

## الوَكالَةُ

٣٧٥. كانَ النَّبِيُّ ﷺ يُوَكِّلُ فِي حوائجه الخاصة، وحوائج المسلمين المتعلقة به.

٣٧٦. فهي عقد جائز من الطرفين.

٣٧٧. تدخل في جميع الأشياء التي تصح النيابة فيها:

أ- من حقوق الله: كتفريق الزكاة، والكفارة، ونحوها.

ب- ومن حقوق الآدميين: كالعقود والفسوخ، وغيرها.

٣٧٨. وما لا تدخله النيابة من الأمور التي تتعين على الإنسان وتتعلق ببدنه خاصة؛ كالصلاة، والطهارة، والحلف، والقسم بين الزوجات، ونحوها: لا تجوز الوكالة فيها.

**379.** The agent is not allowed to administer that which he was not given permission for, either verbally or according to custom.

**380.** It is permissible to appoint an agent by *ju'l* (A contract in which the entitlement to wages depends upon the completion of the task.)

**381.** The agent is like all bearers of trusts; he is not legally liable except in the case of transgression or negligence.

**382.** His statement in this regard is accepted with an oath.

**383.** If a representative claims to have returned what he was entrusted with:

1. If he was appointed by *ju'l,* his statement will not be accepted unless he has clear proof (*bayyinah*).
2. If he was a volunteer, his statement will be accepted with an oath.

**(Partnership)**

**384.** The Prophet ﷺ said, "Allāh ﷻ says, 'I am the third [partner] of two partners as long as one of them does not cheat his companion; and if he cheats, I depart from both of them." (Abū Dāwūd)

٣٧٩. ولا يَتَصَرَّفُ الوَكِيلُ في غَيرِ ما أُذِنَ لَه فيه نطقًا أو عرفًا.

٣٨٠. ويجوز التَّوْكِيلُ بِجُعْل أو غَيْرِهِ.

٣٨١. وهُوَ كَسائِرِ الأُمَناءِ، لا ضَمانَ عَلَيْهِمْ إلّا بِالتَّعَدِّي أوِ التَّفْرِيطِ.

٣٨٢. ويُقْبَلُ قَوْلُهُمْ في عَدَمِ ذَلِكَ بِاليَمِينِ.

٣٨٣. ومَنِ ادَّعى الرَّدَّ مِنَ الأُمَناءِ:

١. فإنْ كانَ بِجُعْلٍ، لَمْ يُقْبَلْ إلّا بِبَيِّنَةٍ،

٢. وإنْ كانَ مُتَبَرِّعًا، قُبِلَ قَوْلُهُ بِيَمِينِه.

## الشَّرِكَة

٣٨٤. وقال ﷺ: «يَقُولُ اللهُ تَعالى: أنا ثالِثُ الشَّرِيكَيْنِ ما لَمْ يَخُنْ أحَدُهُما صاحِبَهُ، فإذا خانَهُ خَرَجْتُ مِن بَيْنِهِما» رَواهُ أبُو داوُدَ

**385.** All forms of partnership are non-binding.

**386.** Ownership and profit is in accordance to what they agree upon as long as it is a known and specific percentage.

**387.** The types of partnership are:

1. *Sharikah al ʿInān:* (Cooperative Partnership). This is where both partners invest with capital and labour.
2. *Sharikah al Muḍārabah:* (Silent Partnership). This is where one of the partners invests with capital and the other partner bears the labour.
3. *Sharikah al Wujūh:* (Reputable Partnership). This is where both partners purchase trade goods for a deferred payment based upon their repute.
4. *Sharikah al Abdān:* (Manual Partnership). This is where both partners share what they earn by their own work from permissible trade like cutting grass etc.
5. *Sharikah al Mufāwaḍah:* (Comprehensive Partnership). This is a comprehensive partnership that covers all types of partnerships mentioned.

**388.** All forms of these aforementioned partnerships are permissible.

٣٨٥. فالشركة بجميع أنواعها كلها جائزة

٣٨٦. ويَكُونُ المِلْكُ فِيها والرِّبْحُ بِحَسْبِ ما يَتَّفِقانِ عَلَيْهِ، إذا كانَ جُزْءًا مُشاعًا مَعْلُومًا.

٣٨٧. فَدَخَلَ في هذا:

١. شَرِكَةُ العِنانِ، وهِيَ: أنْ يَكُونَ مِن كلٍّ مِنهُما مالٌ وعَمَلٌ.

٢. وشَرِكَةُ المضارَبَةِ: بِأنْ يَكُونَ مِن أحَدِهِما المالُ ومِن الآخَرِ العَمَلُ.

٣. وشَرِكَةُ الوُجُوهِ: بِما يَأْخُذانِ بِوُجُوهِهِما مِن النّاسِ.

٤. وشَرِكَةُ الأبْدانِ: بِأنْ يَشْتَرِكا بِما يَكْتَسِبانِ بِأبْدانِهِما مِن المُباحاتِ مِن حَشِيشٍ ونَحْوِهِ، وما يَتَقَبَّلانِهِ مِن الأعْمالِ.

٥. وشَرِكَةُ المفاوَضَةِ: وهِيَ الجامِعَةُ لِجَمِيعِ ذَلِكَ،

٣٨٨. وكُلُّها جائِزَةٌ.

**389.** However, they will become null and void if either of the partners were to be unjust or acted ambiguously, such as if one were to take profit for a specific time period and the other partner were to take the profit for another time period. Or if one were to take the profit for one commodity and the other take the profit from another commodity, or if one were to take the profit from one journey and the other take the profit from another journey, and so on.

**390.** Crop sharing also becomes null and void if there were any injustice or ambiguity.

Rāfiʿ bin Khadīj ﷺ said, "People used to let out land in the time of the Messenger of Allāh ﷺ for what grew by the current of water and at the banks of streamlets and at the places of cultivation. Sometimes this [portion] perished and that [portion] was saved, and sometimes this remained intact and that perished. There was no [form of] lease among the people except this. Therefore, he forbade it. But if there is something which is secure and known, then there is no harm in it. (Muslim)

Moreover, the Prophet ﷺ made a contract with the people of *Khaibar* that they could utilise the land on condition that he would take half of the fruits or cultivation. (Agreed upon)

٣٨٩. ويُفْسِدُها إذا دَخَلَها الظُّلْمُ والغَرَرُ لِأَحَدِهِما، كَأَنْ يَكُونَ لِأَحَدِهِما رِبْحُ وقْتٍ مُعَيَّنٍ، وِللْآخَرِ رِبْحُ وقْتٍ آخَرَ، أوْ رِبْحُ إحْدى السِّلْعَتَيْنِ، أوْ إحْدى السَّفْرَتَيْنِ، وما يُشْبِهُ ذَلِكَ.

٣٩٠. كما يفسد ذلك المساقاة والمزارعة.

وقالَ رافِعُ بْنُ خَدِيجٍ: وكانَ النّاسُ يُؤاجِرُونَ على عهد رسول الله ﷺ ما عَلى الماذِياناتِ، وأقْبالِ الجَداوِلِ، وشَيْءٌ مِن الزَّرْعِ، فَيَهْلِكُ هَذا ويَسْلَمُ هَذا، ويَسْلَمُ هَذا ويَهْلِكُ هَذا، ولَمْ يَكُنْ لِلنّاسِ كِراءٌ إلّا هَذا، فَلِذَلِكَ زَجَرَ عَنْهُ. فَأمّا شَيْءٌ مَعْلُومٌ مَضْمُونٌ، فَلا بَأْسَ بِهِ. رَواهُ مُسْلِمٌ.

وعامل النبي ﷺ أهْلَ خَيْبَرَ بِشَطْرِ ما يَخْرُجُ منها من ثمر أو زرع. متفق عليه

**391.** *Al Musāqāh* (watering) of trees is when one gives a labourer a tree to take care of in return for a specified share of the fruits of the tree.

**392.** *Al Muzāraʿah* (crop sharing) is when one gives a person a piece of land to cultivate and is then given a specific share of the produce.

**393.** Both types of crop sharing should be in accordance to what is customarily considered to be correct on condition that there is no ambiguity.

**394.** If a person gives another his animal to work with, any agreement between the two (about the sharing of earnings) is permissible.

٣٩١. فالمساقاة عَلى الشَّجَرِ: بِأَنْ يَدْفَعَها لِلْعامِلِ، ويَقُومَ عَلَيْها، بجزء مشاع معلوم من الثمرة.

٣٩٢. والمزارعة: بأن يدفع الأرض لمن يزرعها بجزء مشاع معلوم من الزرع.

٣٩٣. وعَلى كُلٍّ مِنهُما: ما جَرَتِ العادَةُ بِهِ، والشَّرطُ الذِي لا جَهالَةَ فِيهِ.

٣٩٤. ولَوْ دَفَعَ دابة إلى آخَرَ يَعْمَلُ عَلَيْها، وما حَصَلَ بَيْنَهُما: جاز.

بَابُ إِحْيَاءِ المَوَات

# Chapter: Cultivation of Barren Lands

**395.** *Mawāt* refers to uncultivated land which has no known owner.

**396.** Whoever brings life back to it, such as by building a wall around it, digging a well in it, supplying water to it, andremoving that which makes land infertile, qualifies to own the land and that what is in it, with exception to metals that do not require to be excavated. This is based upon the *ḥadīth* narrated by Ibn ʿUmar ﷺ, "Whoever cultivates land that does not belong to anyone is more entitled to it." (Bukhārī)

**397.** If one were to surround barren land with stones or dig a well that did not reach water or is given land (from an official authority) is more entitled to it. However, he cannot own it until he cultivates it through the aforementioned means.

# بابُ إحْياءِ المَواتِ

٣٩٥. وهِيَ الأرْضُ البائِرَةُ التي لا يُعْلَم لها مَالِك.

٣٩٦. فَمَن أحْياها بِحائِطٍ، أوْ حَفْرِ بِئْرٍ، أوْ إجْراءِ ماءٍ إلَيْها، أوْ مَنع ما لا تُزْرَعُ مَعَهُ: مَلَكَها بِجَميعِ ما فيها، إلّا المعادِنَ الظّاهِرَةَ؛ لِحَديثِ ابْنِ عُمَرَ: «مَن أحْيا أرْضًا لَيْسَتْ لِأحَدٍ فَهُوَ حَقُّ بِها» رَواهُ البُخاريُّ

٣٩٧. وإذا تَحَجَّرَ مَواتًا: بِأنْ أدارَ حَوْلَهُ أحْجارًا، أوْ حَفَرَ بِئْرًا لَمْ يَصِلْ إلى مائِها، أوْ أُقطِع أرْضًا: فَهُوَ أحَقُّ بِها، ولا يَمْلِكُها حَتّى يُحْيِيَها بما تقدم.

بابُ الجعَالَة والإجَارَة

# Chapter: Job Wages & Hiring

398. Both [terms] refer to the remuneration given to a person in exchange for a known amount of work (*ijārah*), or an unknown amount of work in the case of *jaʿālah* (wages). Or, for a *manfaʿah* (service) while in possession of it and being responsible for it.

399. Whoever carries out what the remuneration is set for, in both cases, deserves to be paid. Whoever does not, does not deserve to be paid.

400. The exception to this is if the person was unable to complete the work in the case of *ijārah*. In such a case, he is paid in ratio to what he has done.

401. Abu Hurayrah ﷺ narrated that the Prophet ﷺ said, "Allāh ﷻ says, 'I will be against three people on the Day of Resurrection: one who makes a covenant in my name, but he proves treacherous; one who sells a free person into slavery and profits from it; and one who employs a labourer and receives the requested work but does not pay him his wages.'" (Muslim)

# بابُ الجَعالَةِ والإجارَةِ

٣٩٨. وهُمَا: جَعْلُ مالٍ مَعْلُومٍ لِمَن يَعْمَلُ لَهُ عَمَلًا مَعْلُومًا، أوْ مَجْهُولًا فِي الجَعالَةِ، ومَعْلُومًا فِي الإجارَةِ، أوْ عَلَى مَنفَعَةٍ فِي الذِّمَّةِ.

٣٩٩. فَمَن فَعَلَ ما جُعِلَ عليه فيهما، استحق العوض، وإلا فلا.

٤٠٠. إلا إذا تعذر العمل في الإجارة، فإنه يتقسط العوض.

٤٠١. وعَنْ أبي هُرَيْرَةَ مَرْفُوعًا: ﴿قالَ اللَّهُ تَعالى: ثَلاثَةٌ أنا خَصْمُهُمْ يَوْمَ القِيامَةِ: رَجُلٌ أعْطى بِي ثُمَّ غَدَرَ، ورَجُلٌ باعَ حُرًّا فَأَكَلَ ثَمَنَهُ، ورَجُلٌ اسْتَأْجَرَ أجِيرًا فاسْتَوْفى مِنهُ ولَمْ يُعْطِهِ أجْرَهُ﴾ رَواهُ مُسْلِمٌ

**402.** Ja'ālah is broader than ijārah, as it is permissible for charitable deeds. Furthermore, unlike ijārah, the type of work involved can be known or unknown and it is a non-binding type of transaction.

**403.** It is permissible to sublease something already hired to one in similar circumstances but not to someone who would cause more harm if done so.

**404.** Neither of the two will be liable unless there is negligence or transgression.

**405.** The Prophet ﷺ said, "Give the worker his earnings before his sweat dries." (Ibn Mājah)

٤٠٢. والجعالَةُ أوْسَعُ مِن الإجارَةِ؛ لأنَّها تَجُوزُ عَلى أعْمالِ القُرب، ولأنَّ العَمَلَ فيها يَكُونُ مَعْلُومًا ومَجْهُولًا، ولأنَّها عَقْدٌ جائِزٌ، بِخِلافِ الإجارَةِ.

٤٠٣. وتَجُوزُ إجارَةُ العَيْنِ المؤَجَّرَةِ لِمَن يَقُومُ مَقامَهُ، لا بِأكْثَرَ مِنهُ ضَرَرًا.

٤٠٤. ولا ضَمانَ فِيهِما، بِدُونِ تعدٍّ ولا تَفْرِيطٍ

# بابُ اللُّقَطَة واللَّقِيط

# Chapter: Found Property & the Foundling

**406.** There are three types of lost and found property:

1. That which is insignificant in value, such as a whip or bread. These things can be claimed and owned without needing to announce it (ta'rīf).

2. Stray animals that can defend themselves against small predators such as camels. Such cannot be taken in any circumstance.

3. Anything other than the above. It is allowed for one to pick up this type of item on condition that they announce it for a entire year, after which they can take ownership of it.

On the authority of Zayd bin Khālid al-Juhani, "A man came to the Prophet ﷺ and asked him about a lost piece of property. He said, "Familiarise yourself with its container and tying material and then publicly announce it for a year. If its owner appears [then return it to him], otherwise use it as you like." The man then said, "What about a lost sheep?" To which he ﷺ replied, "It is [either] for you, your brother, or a wolf."

# بابُ اللُّقَطَةِ واللَّقيطِ

٤٠٦. وهِيَ عَلى ثَلاثَةِ أَضْرُبٍ:

أَحَدُها: ما تَقِلُّ قِيمَتُهُ، كالسَّوْطِ والرَّغيفِ ونَحْوِهما، فَيُمْلَكُ بِلا تَعْريفٍ.

والثّاني: الضَّوالُّ التي تَمْتَنِعُ مِن صِغارِ السِّباعِ، كالإِبِلِ، فَلا تُمْلَكُ بِالالتِقاطِ مُطْلَقًا.

والثّالِثُ: ما سِوى ذَلِكَ، فَيَجُوزُ الْتِقاطُهُ، ويَمْلِكُهُ إذا عَرَّفَهُ سَنَةً كامِلَةً.

وعَنْ زَيْدِ بْنِ خالِدٍ الجُهَنِيِّ ﷺ، قال: جاء رجل إلى النبي ﷺ فسأله عن اللقطة، فقال: «اعرف عِفاصها ووكاءَها، ثم عَرِّفها سنة، فإن جاء صاحبها، وإلا فشأنُكَ بها».

قال: فضالة الغنم؟ قال: «هي لك أو لأخيك أو للذئب»،

The man then said, "What about a stray camel?" To which he ﷺ replied, "Why should you take it when it has its water container (i.e. its stomach) and its hooves and can reach water and eat plants until the owner finds it?" (Agreed upon)

**407.** Picking up the foundling (*laqīṭ*) and taking care of him/her is a communal obligation.

**408.** If the *Bayt al Māl* (treasury) is unable to see to this, then it is incumbent upon the one who knows the circumstances of the foundling to see to him/her.

قال: فضالة الإبل؟ قال: «ما لك ولها؟ معها سقاؤها وحذاؤها، ترد الماء، وتأكل الشجر، حتى يلقاها ربُّها».

مُتَّفَقٌ عَلَيْهِ.

٤٠٧. والْتِقاطُ اللَّقِيطِ، والقِيامُ بِهِ: فَرْضُ كِفايَةٍ.

٤٠٨. فَإِنْ تَعَذَّرَ بيتُ المالِ فَعَلى مَن علم بحاله.

# بَابُ المُسَابَقَة والمُغَالَبَة

# Chapter: Competition & Wrestling

**409.** There are three types [of competition]:

1. Permissible with a prize or reward. This applies to horse and camel racing, and archery.

2. Permissible without a prize and prohibited with a prize. These are all competitions other than the above-mentioned three.

3. Dice, chess, and the like. These are prohibited in all cases. This is as per the hadith, "There should be no prizes for competitions except for competitions for races with camels, arrows and horses." (Aḥmad)

**410.** Anything other than the aforementioned falls under gambling.

# بابُ المُسابقَةِ والمُغالَبَةِ

٤٠٩. وهِيَ ثَلاثَةُ أنْواعٍ:

نَوْعٌ: يَجُوزُ بِعِوَضٍ وغَيْرِهِ، وهِيَ: مُسابَقَةُ الخَيْلِ والإِبِلِ والسهام.

ونوعٌ: يَجُوزُ بِلا عِوَضٍ، ولا يَجُوزُ بِعِوَضٍ، وهِيَ: جَمِيعُ المغالباتِ بِغَيْرِ الثَّلاثَةِ المذْكُورَةِ، وبِغَيْرِ النَّرْدِ والشَّطْرَنْج ونَحْوِهِما، فَتُحَرَّمُ مُطْلَقًا، وهُوَ النَّوْعُ الثَّالِثُ؛ لِحَدِيثِ: «لا سَبَقَ إلّا فِي خُفٍّ أوْ نَصْلٍ أوْ حافِرٍ» رَواهُ أَحْمَدُ والثَّلاثَةُ.

٤١٠. وأمّا ما سِواها: فَإِنَّها داخِلَةٌ فِي القِمارِ والمَيْسِرِ.

بَابُ الغَصْب

# Chapter: Usurpation

**411.** *Ghaṣb* is defined as seizing another person's property without any right.

**412.** It is prohibited as per the *ḥadīth*, "Whoever usurps a hand-span of land will bear seven earths on the Day of Resurrection." (Agreed upon)

**413.** The usurper must return what was taken to its owner, even if it costs more than the value of what was usurped.

**414.** He is also liable for any depreciation in its value as well as the cost of its hire while it was in his hands. He is also liable for any damage or destruction.

**415.** Any growth from the usurped property belongs to its rightful owner.

**416.** If the usurped property was a piece of land and the usurper planted something in it or built something on it, then the rightful owner has a right to remove it as per the *ḥadīth*, "The sweat of an unjust person has no right." (Abū Dāwūd)

# بابُ الغَصْبِ

٤١١. وهُوَ الِاسْتِيلَاءُ عَلى مالِ الغَيْرِ بِغَيْرِ حَقٍّ.

٤١٢. وهُوَ مُحَرَّمٌ، لِحَدِيثِ: «مَن اِقْتَطَعَ شِبْرًا مِن الأرْضِ ظُلْمًا طَوَّقَهُ اللَّهُ بِهِ يَوْمَ القِيامَةِ مِن سَبْعِ أرْضِينَ». مُتَّفَقٌ عَلَيْهِ.

٤١٣. وعَلَيْهِ: رَدُّهُ لِصاحِبِهِ، ولَوْ غرم أضعافه.

٤١٤. وعَلَيْهِ: نَقْصُهُ وأُجْرَتُهُ مُدَّةَ مُقامِهِ بِيَدِهِ، وضمانُه إذا تلف مطلقًا.

٤١٥. وزيادته لربه.

٤١٦. وإنْ كانَتْ أرْضًا فَغَرَسَ أوْ بَنى فِيها، فَلِرَبِّه قلعُه؛ لِحَدِيثِ «لَيْسَ لِعِرْقٍ ظالِمٍ حَقٌّ» رواه أبو داود

**417.** Whoever takes possession of an item from its usurper whilst knowing about its usurpation is subject to the same ruling as that of the usurper.

٤١٧. ومَنْ انْتَقَلَتْ إِلَيْهِ العَيْنُ مِن الغَاصِبِ، وَهُوَ عَالِمٌ، فَحُكْمُهُ حُكْمُ الغَاصِب.

بَابُ العَارِيَّة والوَدِيعَة

# Chapter: Lending Items and Trusts

**(Lending Items)**

**418.** *Al ʿĀriyyah* is defined as permitting someone to benefit from something.

**419.** It is recommended since it is considered to be from *iḥsān* (beneficence) and *maʿrūf* (kindness). The Prophet ﷺ said, "Every act of kindness is a form of charity." (Agreed upon)

**420.** If the lender stipulates compensation for its loss or damage, the borrower will be liable.

**421.** If the borrower was to transgress or be negligent, then he will have to compensate, otherwise he does not have to.

**(Trusts)**

**422.** Whoever was entrusted with a trust must safeguard it in a place that is adequately safe for it.

**423.** The entrusted person is not allowed to benefit from the trust without permission from its rightful owner.

# بابُ العارِيةِ والوَديعةِ

## [الْعارِيَّةُ]

٤١٨. العارِيَّةُ: إباحةُ المنافعِ.

٤١٩. وهِيَ مُستَحَبَّةٌ لِدُخُولِها في الإحسانِ والمعْرُوفِ.

قالَ ﷺ: «كُلُّ مَعْرُوفٍ صَدَقةٌ».

٤٢٠. وإنْ شرطِ ضمانُها ضَمِنَها.

٤٢١. أوْ تَعَدَّى أوْ فَرَّطَ فِيها، ضَمِنَها، وإلّا فَلا.

## [الوَديعةِ]

٤٢٢. ومَن أُودع وديعةً فعَلَيهِ حَفِظُها في حِرْزِ مِثْلِها.

٤٢٣. ولا ينتفع بها بغير إذن ربها.

77

# بَابُ الشُّفْعَة

# Chapter: Pre-emption

**424.** It is defined as: A person's right to take his partner's share that was transferred to another person by a sale or other means.

**425.** It applies to property that has not been divided as per the *ḥadīth* of Jābir 🙵, "The Prophet 🙵 established the right of pre-emption [to the partner] in everything that cannot be divided, but if the boundaries of the property were demarcated or the ways and streets were fixed, then there is pre-emption." (Agreed upon)

**426.** The use of loopholes or trickery is not permitted to evade it.

**427.** Is someone employed trickery, the pre-emption will not be averted as per the *ḥadīth*, "Actions are judged by their intentions."

# بابُ الشُّفْعَةِ

٤٢٤. وهِيَ: اِسْتِحْقاقُ الإِنْسانِ اِنْتِزاعَ حِصَّةِ شَرِيكِهِ مِن يَدِ مَنِ اِنْتَقَلَتْ إِلَيْهِ بِبَيْعٍ ونحوه.

٤٢٥. وهِيَ خاصَّةٌ فِي العَقارِ الذِي لَمْ يُقَسَّمْ؛ لِحَدِيثِ جابِرٍ رضي الله عنه: «قَضى النَّبِيُّ ﷺ بِالشُّفْعَةِ فِي كُلِّ ما لَمْ يُقَسَّمْ، فَإذا وقَعَتِ الحُدُودُ وصُرِّفَتِ الطُّرُقُ فَلا شُفْعَةَ» مُتَّفَقٌ عَلَيْهِ.

٤٢٦. ولا يَحِلُّ التحيل لإسقاطها.

٤٢٧. فَإِنْ تَحَيَّلَ لَمْ تَسْقُطْ؛ لِحَدِيثِ: «إنَّما الأَعْمالُ بالنيات».

79

بَابُ الوَقْف

# Chapter: Endowments

**428.** It is defined as the retention of any property that can be benefited from and dedicating it to charitable purposes.

**429.** It is considered to be from the best and most beneficial deeds to Allāh ﷻ if done out of piety, free from injustice, as per the ḥadīth, "When a servant dies, his actions discontinue except three things: recurring charity, knowledge by which benefit is acquired, or a pious child who prays for him." (Muslim)

Ibn ʿUmar ﷺ also narrated that, "ʿUmar ﷺ acquired a land at *Khaibar*. He came to the Prophet ﷺ and sought his advice in regard to it. He said, "Allāh's Messenger, I have acquired land in *Khaibar*. I have never acquired property more valuable for me than this, so what do you command me to do with it?" Thereupon he ﷺ said, "If you like, you may keep the corpus intact and give its produce as ṣadaqah." So ʿUmar ﷺ gave it as ṣadaqah, declaring that the property must not be sold or inherited or given away as gift. ʿUmar ﷺ devoted it to the poor, the nearest kin, the emancipation of slaves, those in the way of Allāh ﷻ and guests.

# بابُ الوَقْفِ

٤٢٨. وهُوَ تَحْبِيسُ الأصْلِ وتَسْبِيلَ المنافِعِ.

٤٢٩. وهو من أفْضَلُ القُرَب وأنْفَعُها إذا كانَ عَلى جِهَةِ بر، وسلم من الظلم؛ لحديث: ﴿إذا مات العبد انقطع عمله إلا من ثلاث: صدقةٍ جارية، أو علمٍ ينتفع به، أو ولدٍ صالح يدعو له﴾ رواهُ مُسْلِمُ.

وعَنْ ابْنِ عُمَرَ قالَ: أصابَ عمرُ أرْضًا بِخَيْبَرَ، فأتى النَّبِيَّ ﷺ يَسْتَأْمِرُهُ فِيها. فقالَ: يا رَسُولَ اللهِ، إنّي أصَبْتُ أرْضًا بخيبرَ لَمْ أُصِبْ مالًا قَطُّ هُوَ أنْفَسُ عِنْدِي مِنهُ، قالَ: ﴿إنْ شِئْتَ حَبَّسْتَ أصلَها وتَصَدَّقْتَ بِها﴾، قالَ: فَتَصَدَّقَ بِها عُمَرُ، غَيْرَ أنَّهُ لا يُباعُ أصْلُها ولا يُورَثُ ولا يُوهَبُ، فتَصَدَّقَ بِها في الفُقَراءِ، وفِي القُرْبى، وفِي الرِّقابِ، وفِي سَبِيلِ اللهِ، وابْنِ السَّبِيلِ، والضَّيْفِ،

There is no sin for one who administers it if he consumes something from it in a reasonable manner or if he feeds his friends and does not hoard up goods [for himself]." Agreed upon.

**430.** The best type of endowment is that which is more beneficial to the Muslims.

**431.** It comes into effect by a meaningful statement expressing the wish to make the endowment.

**432.** The conditions of the endowment and how it should be used should be in accordance with the conditions laid down by the endower as long as they confine to Islamic law.

**433.** It should not be sold unless it stops providing benefit, in which case it should be sold, and its returns should be used for something similar to it.

لا جُناحَ عَلى مَن وليَها أَنْ يَأْكُلَ مِنها بِالمَعْرُوفِ، ويُطْعِمَ صَدِيقًا، غَيْرَ مُتَمَوِّلٍ مالًا.» مُتَّفَقٌ عَلَيْهِ.

٤٣٠. وأَفْضَلُهُ أَنْفَعُهُ لِلْمُسْلِمِينَ.

٤٣١. ويَنْعَقِدُ بِالقَوْلِ الدَّالِّ عَلى الوَقْفِ.

٤٣٢. ويُرْجعُ في مَصارِفِ الوَقْفِ وشُرُوطه إلى شرط الواقف حيث وافق الشرع.

٤٣٣. ولا يباع إلا أن تتعطل منافعه، فيباع، ويجعل في مثله، أو بعض مثله.

بَابُ الهِبَة والعَطِيَّة والوَصِيَّة

# Chapter: Gifts, Bestowals & Bequests

**434.** These are considered to be contracts of gratuity.

**435.** A *hibah* (gift) is wealth donated whilst one is alive and healthy.

**436.** An *ʿaṭiyyah* (bestowal) is wealth donated when one is terminally ill or close to death.

**437.** A *waṣiyyah* (bequest) is wealth donated after death.

**438.** All the aforementioned are acts of beneficence and piety.

**439.** A *hibah* is taken from one's capital (with no limit).

**440.** An *ʿaṭiyyah* and a *waṣiyyah* is taken from a third or less of one's capital for other than an heir.

**441.** Anything more than a third, or that given to an heir, will be dependent upon the permission of the heirs that which are of sound mind.

# بابُ الهِبةِ والعَطيَّةِ والوَصيَّةِ

٤٣٤. وهِيَ مِن عُقُودِ التَّبَرُّعاتِ.

٤٣٥. فالهِبةُ: التَّبَرُّعُ بالمالِ في حالِ الحَياةِ والصحة.

٤٣٦. والعَطِيَّةُ: التَّبَرُّعُ بهِ في مَرَضِ مَوْتِهِ المخُوف.

٤٣٧. والوصية: التبرع بهِ بَعْدَ الوَفاةِ.

٤٣٨. فالجَمِيعُ داخِلٌ في الإحْسانِ والبِرِّ.

٤٣٩. فالهِبَةُ مِن رَأْسِ المالِ.

٤٤٠. والعَطِيَّةِ والوَصِيَّةَ مِن الثُّلُثِ فأَقَلُّ لِغَيْرِ وارِثٍ،

٤٤١. فَما زادَ عَنْ الثُّلُثِ، أوْ كانَ لِوارِثٍ تَوَقَّفَ على إجازَةِ الوَرثَةِ المرْشدِينَ.

**442.** It is obligatory to be just with one's children when dealing with the above as per the *ḥadīth*, "Be conscious of Allāh 🕌 and be fair towards your children." (Agreed upon)

**443.** After a gift has been taken possession of and accepted, it is unlawful for the giver to take it back as per the *ḥadīth*, "The one who takes back his gift, is like the dog which vomits then goes back to its vomit." (Agreed upon)

In another *ḥadīth* it states, "It is not lawful for anyone that has given a gift to take it back, except for a father who gives something to his son." (Abū Dāwūd)

**444.** The Prophet 🕌 used to accept gifts and reciprocate the giver.

**445.** The father has the right to take ownership of his child's wealth as long as it does not harm the child or gives it to another son or take it whilst one of them is about to die as per the *ḥadīth*, "You and your wealth belong to your father." (Abū Dāwūd)

**446.** Ibn ʿUmar 🕌 narrated in a *marfūʿ ḥadīth*, "It is the duty of a Muslim man who has something which is to be given as bequest not to have it for two nights without having his will written regarding it." (Agreed upon)

٤٤٢. وكُلُّها يَجِبُ فِيها العَدْلُ بَيْنَ أَوْلادِهِ؛ لِحَدِيثٍ: «اِتَّقُوا اللَّهَ واعْدِلُوا بَيْنَ أَوْلادِكُمْ» مُتَّفَقٌ عَلَيْهِ.

٤٤٣. وبَعْدَ تَقْبِيضِ الهِبَةِ وقَبُولِها لا يَحِلُّ الرجوع فِيها لِحَدِيثٍ: «العائِدُ فِي هِبَتِهِ كالكَلْبِ يَقِيءُ ثُمَّ يَعُودُ فِي قَيْئِهِ» مُتَّفَقٌ عَلَيْهِ، وفِي الحَدِيثِ الآخَرِ: «لا يَحِلُّ لِرَجُلٍ مُسْلِمٍ أَنْ يُعْطِيَ العَطِيَّةَ ثُمَّ يَرْجِعَ فِيها؛ إِلَّا الوالِدِ فِيما يُعْطِي لِوَلَدِهِ» رَواهُ أَهْلُ السُّنَنِ.

٤٤٤. وكانَ النَّبِيُّ ﷺ يَقْبَلُ الهَدِيَّةَ، ويُثِيبُ عليها.

٤٤٥. ولِلْأَبِ أَنْ يَتَمَلَّكَ مِن مالِ ولَدِهِ ما شاءَ، ما لَمْ يَضُرُّهُ، أَوْ يُعْطِيهِ لِوَلَدٍ آخَر، أَوْ يَكُونَ بِمَرَضٍ مَوْتِ أَحَدِهِما؛ لِحَدِيثٍ: «أنت ومالك لأبيك».

٤٤٦. وعن ابن عمر مرفوعًا: «ما حَقُّ امرئٍ مُسْلِمٍ لَهُ شَيْءٌ يُرِيدُ أَنْ يُوصِي فِيهِ، يَبِيتُ لَيْلَتَيْنِ، إِلا ووصَيَّته مَكْتُوبَةٌ عِنْدَهُ» مُتَّفَقٌ عَلَيْهِ

**447.** In another *ḥadīth* the Prophet ﷺ said, "Allāh ﷻ has appointed for everyone who has a right what is due to him, so no bequest should be made to an heir." (Abū Dāwūd and others) In a variant narration it says, "...unless the heirs consent." (Dāraqutnī)

**448.** One who does not own enough to enrich his heirs should not bequest, rather he should leave all of his wealth to them, since the Prophet ﷺ said, "...It is better for you to leave your heirs wealthy than to leave them poor, begging others..." (Agreed upon)

Seeking well for others is sought in all circumstances.

٤٤٧. وَفِي الحَدِيثِ: «إِنَّ اللَّهَ قَدْ أَعْطَى كُلَّ ذِي حَقٍّ حَقَّهُ، فَلا وَصِيَّةَ لِوَارِثٍ» رَوَاهُ أَهْلُ السُّنَنِ، وَفِي لَفْظٍ: «إِلَّا أن يشاء الورثة»

٤٤٨. وَيَنْبَغِي لِمَن لَيْسَ عِنْدَهُ شَيْءٌ يَحْصُلُ فِيهِ إِغْنَاءُ وَرَثَتِهِ أَنْ لا يُوصِيَ، بَلْ يَدَعَ التَّرِكَةَ كُلَّها لورثته؛ كما قال النبي ﷺ: «إنك إن تذر ورثتك أغنياء خير من أن تذرهم عالة يتكففون الناس» مُتَّفَقٌ عَلَيْهِ. والخَيْرُ مَطْلُوبٌ فِي جَمِيعِ الأَحْوَالِ.

# كِتَابُ المَوَارِيث

# The Book of Inheritance

**449.** *Mawārīth* refers to the knowledge of how to distribute one's estate and those entitled to it.

**450.** It is based on verses from *Sūrah al-Nisāʾ*:

*"Concerning your children, God commands you that a son should have the equivalent share of two daughters. If there are only daughters, two or more should share two-thirds of the inheritance if [only] one, she should have half. Parents inherit a sixth each if the deceased leaves children; if he leaves no children and his parents are his sole heirs, his mother has a third, unless he has brothers, in which case she has a sixth. [In all cases, the distribution comes] after payment of any bequests or debts. You cannot know which of your parents or your children is more beneficial to you: this is a law from God, and He is all knowing, all wise.*

*You inherit half of what your wives leave if they have no children; if they have children, you inherit a quarter. [In all cases, the distribution comes] after payment of any bequests or debts. If you have no children, your wives' share is a quarter; if you have children, your wives receive an eighth. [In all cases, the distribution comes] after payment of any bequests or debts.*

# كِتابُ المَوارِيثِ

٤٤٩. وهِيَ العِلمَ بِقِسمَةِ التَّرِكَةِ بَيْنَ مُسْتَحِقِّيها.

٤٥٠- والأصلُ فيها:

قَوْلُهُ تَعالى ﴿ يُوصِيكُمُ ٱللَّهُ فِىٓ أَوْلَٰدِكُمْ لِلذَّكَرِ مِثْلُ حَظِّ ٱلْأُنثَيَيْنِ فَإِن كُنَّ نِسَآءً فَوْقَ ٱثْنَتَيْنِ فَلَهُنَّ ثُلُثَا مَا تَرَكَ وَإِن كَانَتْ وَٰحِدَةً فَلَهَا ٱلنِّصْفُ وَلِأَبَوَيْهِ لِكُلِّ وَٰحِدٍ مِّنْهُمَا ٱلسُّدُسُ مِمَّا تَرَكَ إِن كَانَ لَهُۥ وَلَدٌ فَإِن لَّمْ يَكُن لَّهُۥ وَلَدٌ وَوَرِثَهُۥٓ أَبَوَاهُ فَلِأُمِّهِ ٱلثُّلُثُ فَإِن كَانَ لَهُۥٓ إِخْوَةٌ فَلِأُمِّهِ ٱلسُّدُسُ مِنۢ بَعْدِ وَصِيَّةٍ يُوصِى بِهَآ أَوْ دَيْنٍ ءَابَآؤُكُمْ وَأَبْنَآؤُكُمْ لَا تَدْرُونَ أَيُّهُمْ أَقْرَبُ لَكُمْ نَفْعًا فَرِيضَةً مِّنَ ٱللَّهِ إِنَّ ٱللَّهَ كَانَ عَلِيمًا حَكِيمًا ۝ وَلَكُمْ نِصْفُ مَا تَرَكَ أَزْوَٰجُكُمْ إِن لَّمْ يَكُن لَّهُنَّ وَلَدٌ فَإِن كَانَ لَهُنَّ وَلَدٌ فَلَكُمُ ٱلرُّبُعُ مِمَّا تَرَكْنَ مِنۢ بَعْدِ وَصِيَّةٍ يُوصِينَ بِهَآ أَوْ دَيْنٍ وَلَهُنَّ ٱلرُّبُعُ مِمَّا تَرَكْتُمْ إِن لَّمْ يَكُن لَّكُمْ وَلَدٌ فَإِن كَانَ لَكُمْ وَلَدٌ فَلَهُنَّ ٱلثُّمُنُ مِمَّا تَرَكْتُم مِّنۢ بَعْدِ وَصِيَّةٍ تُوصُونَ بِهَآ أَوْ دَيْنٍ ﴾

91

*If a man or a woman dies leaving no children or parents, but has a single brother or sister, he or she should take one-sixth of the inheritance; if there are more siblings, they share one-third between them. [In all cases, the distribution comes] after payment of any bequests or debts, with no harm done to anyone: this is a commandment from God: God is all knowing and benign to all.*

*These are the bounds set by God: God will admit those who obey Him and His Messenger to Gardens graced with flowing streams, and there they will stay - that is the supreme triumph!*

*But those who disobey God and His Messenger and overstep His limits will be consigned by God to the Fire, and there they will stay- a humiliating torment awaits them!" (4:11-14)*

Moreover, verse 176 from the same *sūrah* states:

*"They ask you [O Prophet] for a ruling. Say, 'God gives you a ruling about inheritance from someone who dies childless with no surviving parents. If a man leaves a sister, she is entitled to half of the inheritance; if she has no children, her brother is her sole heir; if there are two sisters, they are entitled to two-thirds of the inheritance between them, but if there are surviving brothers and sisters, the male is entitled to twice the share of the female. God makes this clear to you so that you do not make mistakes: He has full knowledge of everything.'"*

وَإِن كَانَ رَجُلٌ يُورَثُ كَلَالَةً أَوِ ٱمْرَأَةٌ وَلَهُۥٓ أَخٌ أَوْ أُخْتٌ فَلِكُلِّ وَٰحِدٍ مِّنْهُمَا ٱلسُّدُسُ فَإِن كَانُوٓاْ أَكْثَرَ مِن ذَٰلِكَ فَهُمْ شُرَكَآءُ فِي ٱلثُّلُثِ مِنۢ بَعْدِ وَصِيَّةٍ يُوصَىٰ بِهَآ أَوْ دَيْنٍ غَيْرَ مُضَآرٍّ وَصِيَّةً مِّنَ ٱللَّهِ وَٱللَّهُ عَلِيمٌ حَلِيمٌ ۝ تِلْكَ حُدُودُ ٱللَّهِ وَمَن يُطِعِ ٱللَّهَ وَرَسُولَهُۥ يُدْخِلْهُ جَنَّٰتٍ تَجْرِي مِن تَحْتِهَا ٱلْأَنْهَٰرُ خَٰلِدِينَ فِيهَا وَذَٰلِكَ ٱلْفَوْزُ ٱلْعَظِيمُ ۝ وَمَن يَعْصِ ٱللَّهَ وَرَسُولَهُۥ وَيَتَعَدَّ حُدُودَهُۥ يُدْخِلْهُ نَارًا خَٰلِدًا فِيهَا وَلَهُۥ عَذَابٌ مُّهِينٌ ۝

[النساء: ١١–١٤]

وَقَوْلِهِ فِي آخِرِ السُّورَةِ: ﴿يَسْتَفْتُونَكَ قُلِ ٱللَّهُ يُفْتِيكُمْ فِي ٱلْكَلَٰلَةِ إِنِ ٱمْرُؤٌاْ هَلَكَ لَيْسَ لَهُۥ وَلَدٌ وَلَهُۥٓ أُخْتٌ فَلَهَا نِصْفُ مَا تَرَكَ وَهُوَ يَرِثُهَآ إِن لَّمْ يَكُن لَّهَا وَلَدٌ فَإِن كَانَتَا ٱثْنَتَيْنِ فَلَهُمَا ٱلثُّلُثَانِ مِمَّا تَرَكَ وَإِن كَانُوٓاْ إِخْوَةً رِّجَالًا وَنِسَآءً فَلِلذَّكَرِ مِثْلُ حَظِّ ٱلْأُنثَيَيْنِ يُبَيِّنُ ٱللَّهُ لَكُمْ أَن تَضِلُّواْ وَٱللَّهُ بِكُلِّ شَيْءٍ عَلِيمٌ

Likewise, Ibn ʿAbbās ﷺ narrated in a *marfūʿ ḥadīth*, "Give the shares of inheritance to those who are entitled to them. As for what remains, then it is for the closet male relative." (Agreed upon)

**451.** These noble verses, in addition to the *ḥadīth* of Ibn ʿAbbās ﷺ, contain most of the rulings of inheritance alongside its details and conditions.

**452.** Allāh ﷻ has decreed that when the following group of people are present, the inheritance is divided amongst themselves: paternal male and female children, grandchildren from a son, full brothers, and paternal brothers.

**453.** Whatever remains after *aṣḥāb al furūḍ* (the legal heirs) have taken their shares is distributed on the basis of the male taking a share equal to two females.

**454.** The aforementioned males take the inheritance or what remains after the legal heirs have taken their shares.

**455.** If there is one daughter, she is entitled to a half.

**456.** If there are two or more, they are entitled to two-thirds.

مَعَ حَدِيثِ اِبْنِ عَبَّاسٍ رضي الله عنهما مَرْفُوعًا: «أَلْحِقُوا الْفَرَائِضِ بِأَهْلِها، فَما بَقِيَ فَلِأَوْلَى رَجُلٍ ذَكَرٍ». مُتَّفَقٌ عَلَيْهِ.

٤٥١. فَقَدِ اِشْتَمَلَتِ الْآيَاتُ الْكَرِيمَةُ مَعَ حَدِيثِ اِبْنِ عَبَّاسٍ عَلى جُلّ أَحْكامِ الْمَوارِيثِ، وذَكَرَها مُفَصَّلَةً بِشُرُوطِها.

٤٥٢. فَجَعَلَ اللَّهُ الذُّكُورَ والإناثَ مِن أَوْلادِ الصُّلْبِ، وأَوْلادِ الِابْنِ، ومِنَ الْإِخْوَةِ الْأَشِقّاءِ، أَوْ لِغَيْرِ أُمٍّ إذا اجتمعوا يقتسمون المال.

٤٥٣. وما أَبْقَتِ الفروض، للذكر مثل حظ الأنثيين.

٤٥٤. وأن الذكور من المذكورين، يأخذون المال، أو ما أبقت الفروض.

٤٥٥. وأن الواحدة من البنات، لها النصف.

٤٥٦. والثنتين فأكثر، لهما الثلثان.

**457.** If there is a daughter and a granddaughter from a son, the daughter is entitled to a half and the granddaughter is entitled to one-sixth, which completes two-thirds.

**458.** The same applies to full sisters or paternal half-sisters in the case of *kalālah* (where the deceased does not leave behind a descendent or ascendant).

**459.** If the deceased's daughters end up taking the entire two-thirds, his granddaughters will not be entitled to anything unless a male is present who is either of the same level of relationship as them or lower.

**460.** Likewise, full sisters prevent half-sisters from the same father from taking anything in the situation where they are not ʿaṣabah (residual heirs) due to the presence of a brother.

**461.** Half-brothers and half-sisters from the same mother are all entitled to one-sixth if they are one, or a third if there are two or more. The males and females will have an equal share.

**462.** However, they will not inherit anything if there are any *furūʿ* (descendants) or *uṣūl* (male ascendants).

**463.** The husband is entitled to half if there are no children from his wife, or a quarter in their presence.

٤٥٧. وإذا كانت بنتٌ وبنتُ ابنٍ، فَلِلْبِنْتِ النصف، ولبنت الابن السدس تكملة الثلثين.

٤٥٨. وَكَذَلِكَ الْأَخَواتِ الشَّقِيقاتِ، واللَّاتِي لِلْأَبِ فِي الْكَلالَةِ؛ إذا لَمْ يَكُنْ لَهُ وَلَدٌ ولا والِدٌ.

٤٥٩. وأنَّهُ إذا اِسْتَغْرَقَتِ الْبَناتُ الثُّلْثَيْنِ، سَقَطَ مَن دُونَهُنَّ مِن بَناتِ الابنِ، إذا لَمْ يَعْصِبْهُنَّ ذَكَرٌ بِدَرَجَتِهِنَّ أوْ أَنْزَلَ مِنهُنَّ.

٤٦٠. وَكَذَلِكَ الشَّقِيقاتُ يُسْقِطْنَ الْأَخَواتِ لِلْأَبِ، إذا لَمْ يَعْصِبْهُنَّ أَخُوهُنَّ

٤٦١. وأن الإخوة لأم والأخوات، للواحد منهم السدس، وللاثنين فأكثر الثلث، يُسَوّى بين ذكورهم وإناثهم.

٤٦٢. وأنَّهم لا يرثون مع الفروع مطلقًا، ولا مع الأصول الذكور.

٤٦٣. وأنَّ الزَّوْجَ لَهُ النِّصْفُ مَعَ عَدَمِ أوْلادِ الزَّوْجَةِ، والرُّبْعُ مَعَ وُجُودِهِمْ.

**464.** A wife is entitled to a quarter if the husband has no children, or an eighth in their presence.

**465.** The mother is entitled to a sixth if there are any children, or if there are two or more brothers or sisters. Otherwise, she is entitled to a third in their absence.

**466.** She is entitled to a third of what remains in the case of the presence of her husband and her parents, or the wife and the parents.

**467.** The Prophet ﷺ assigned a sixth for the grandmother in the case where there is no mother. (Abū Dāwūd)

**468.** The father is entitled to a sixth - but no more - in the presence of male offspring.

**469.** He will also be entitled to a sixth in the presence of only daughters, and will take whatever remains after the legal heirs take their shares. This also applies to the grandfather. Both will only inherit via *taʿṣīb* if the deceased left behind no offspring.

٤٦٤ . وأنَّ الزَّوْجَةَ فَأَكْثَر لَها الرُّبُعُ مَعَ عَدَمِ أَوْلادِ الزَّوْجِ، والثُّمُنِ مَعَ وُجُودِهِمْ.

٤٦٥ . وأنَّ الْأُمَّ لَها السُّدُسُ مَعَ أَحَدٍ مِنَ الأَوْلادِ، أَوْ اِثْنَيْنِ فَأَكْثَرَ مِنَ الإِخْوَةِ أَوْ الأَخَواتِ، والثُّلُثُ مَعَ عَدَمِ ذَلِكَ.

٤٦٦ . وأنَّ لَها ثُلُثَ الباقِي فِي: زَوْجٍ وأبَوَيْنِ، أو زوجة وأبوين.

٤٦٧ . وقَدْ جَعَلَ النَّبِيُّ ﷺ للجدة السدس، إذا لم يكن دونَها أم. رَواهُ أَبُو داوُدَ والنَّسائي.

٤٦٨ . وأنَّ لِلْأَبِ السُّدُسَ، لا يَزِيدُ عَلَيْهِ مَعَ الأَوْلادِ الذُّكُورُ.

٤٦٩ . ولَهُ السُّدُسُ مَعَ الإناثِ، فَإِنْ بَقِيَ بَعْدَ فَرْضِهِنَّ شَيْءٍ أَخْذَهُ تَعْصِيبًا وكَذَلِكَ الجَدُّ، وأنَّهُما يَرِثانِ تَعْصِيبًا مَعَ عَدَمِ الأَوْلادِ مُطْلَقًا.

**470.** All males other than the husband and the maternal brother are from the ʿaṣabah (residual heirs). Thus, they are as follows:

1. Full brothers or paternal brothers, and their sons.
2. Full paternal uncles or paternal uncles, and their sons; uncles of the deceased and all ascendant uncles.
3. Sons and grandsons.

**471.** The ruling of the ʿāṣib (residual heir) is as follows:

1. They will inherit the entire estate if there is no other heir.
2. If there is a legal heir (ṣāḥib farḍ), the residual heir will take what remains after the legal heir takes their share.
3. If the shares of the legal heirs cover the entire estate, the residual heir will inherit nothing. However, that cannot happen in the presence of a paternal son or father.

٤٧٠. وَكَذَلِكَ جَمِيعُ الذُّكُورِ غَيْرَ الزَّوْجِ والأخِ مِنَ الأُمِّ عَصَبَاتٌ، وهُمْ:

١. الإخْوَةُ الأشِقَّاءُ، أوْ لِأبٍ، وأبْناؤُهُمْ.

٢. والأعْمامُ الأشقاء أو لأب، وأبناؤهم، أعمام المَيِّتِ، وأعْمامُ أبِيهِ وجَدَّهُ، وإنْ عَلا.

٣. وكَذا البنون وبنوهم.

٤٧١. وحكم العاصب:

١. أن يأخذ المال كله إذا انفرد.

٢. وإن كان معه صاحب فرض أخذ الباقي بعده.

٣. وإذا استغرقت الفروض التركة لم يَبْقَ للعاصب شيء، ولا يمكن أن تستغرق مع ابن الصلب، ولا مع الأب.

**472.** If there are two or more residual heirs, priority is given in the following order:

1. Sons
2. Fathers
3. Brothers and their sons
4. Uncles and their sons
5. Emancipated male slaves and their residual heirs by themselves.

**473.** Priority is given to those who are nearest in relationship to the deceased.

**474.** If they are of the same *jihah* (degree of relationship), priority is given to the one who has closer *manzilah* (blood ties).

**475.** If they are equal in their closeness, priority is given to the one who has the strongest blood ties, i.e. the full blood relationship is given priority over the paternal relationship.

**476.** A sister will not inherit with a residual heir other than the sons and brothers.

٤٧٢ . وإن وجد عاصبان فأكثر فجهات العصوبة على الترتيب الآتي:

١ . بنوة،

٢ . ثم أبوة،

٣ . ثم أخوة وبنوهم،

٤ . ثم أعمام وبَنُوهُمْ،

٥ . ثُمَّ الوَلاءُ وهُوَ المُعْتَقُ، وعَصباته المتَعَصِّبُونَ بأنفسهم.

٤٧٣ . فيقدَّم منهم الأقرب جهة.

٤٧٤ . فإِنْ كانُوا فِي جِهَةٍ واحِدَةٍ، قُدِّمَ الأقْرَبُ مَنزِلَةً.

٤٧٥ . فإِنْ كانُوا فِي المنزِلَةِ سَواءً، قُدِّمَ الأقوى منهم، وهو الشقيق على الذي لأبٍ.

٤٧٦ . وكل عاصبٍ غير الأبناء والإخوة، لا ترث أخته معه شيئًا.

**477.** If the inheritance of the legal heirs exceeds the amount of the estate, and none of them exclude the others from a share, then the issue becomes one of ʿawl, which will mean a percentage of each heir is proportionately decreased as follows:

1. If a person died leaving behind a husband, mother, and non-maternal sister, in which case the denominator is six, the new denominator will increase to eight.
2. The same applies if there was a maternal brother.
3. If there were two brothers, the denominator will increase to nine.
4. If the non-maternal sisters are two, the denominator will increase to ten.
5. If there are two daughters, a mother, and a husband, the denominator would increase from twelve to thirteen.
6. If they are accompanied by the father, the denominator is increased to fifteen.
7. If the deceased left behind two wives, two maternal sisters, two non-maternal sisters, and a mother, the denominator increases to seventeen.
8. If there are two parents, two daughters, and a wife, the denominator increases to twenty-seven.

٤٧٧. وإذا اجتمعت فروضٌ تزيد على المسألة، بحيث يسقط بعضهم بعضًا: عالَتْ بِقَدْرِ فُرُوضِهِمْ:

١. فإذا كانَ زَوْجٌ وأُمٌّ وأُخْتٌ لِغَيْرِ أُمٍّ، فأَصْلُها سِتَّةٌ، وتَعُولُ لَثمانِيَةٍ.

٢. فإنْ كانَ لهُمْ أخٌ لأُمٍّ فَكَذَلِكَ.

٣. فإنْ كانُوا اِثْنَيْنِ، عالَتْ لِتِسْعَةٍ.

٤. فإنْ كانَ الأَخَواتُ لغير أم ثنتين عالت إلى عشرة.

٥. وإذا كانَ بِنْتانِ وأُمٌّ وزَوْجٌ، عالَتْ مِن اثني عشر إلى ثلاثة عشر.

٦. فإن كان معهم أب، عالت إلى خمسة عشر.

٧. فإن خلف زوجتين وأختين لأم وأختين لغيرها وأمًّا، عالت إلى سبعة عَشَرَ.

٨. فإِنْ كانَ أبوانِ وابنَتانِ وزَوْجَةٌ، عالَتْ مِن أَرْبَعَةٍ وعِشْرِينَ إلى سَبْعَةٍ وعِشْرِينَ

**478.** If the legal heirs do not consume the entire inheritance and there are no residual heirs to take the remaining share, the remaining estate is divided amongst the legal heirs according to their percentages.

**479.** If there are no legal heirs and no residual heirs, the estate is inherited by *dhawū al arḥām* (the extended family members who have not been mentioned yet) who in turn take the place of those who were closer to the deceased.

**480.** If someone leaves behind no form of heir, his wealth will go to the treasury and be spent on public and private interests.

**481.** When a person dies, the following four rights should be sufficed first:

1. Burial costs
2. Repaying secured and non-secured loans from the entire capital
3. If a bequest was left behind, up to one third of the estate can be designated to it if the recipients are non-heirs
4. The remaining estate is divided amongst the heirs as explained in this chapter. And Allāh ﷻ knows best

٤٧٨ . وإنْ كانَتِ الفُرُوضُ أَقَلَّ مِنِ المسْألَةِ ولَمْ يَكُنْ معهم عاصب، رُدَّ الفاضل على ذي فرض بقدر فرضه.

٤٧٩ . فإنْ عُدِمَ أَصْحابُ الفُرُوضِ والعَصَباتِ، ورِثَ ذَوُو الأَرْحامِ، وهُمْ مِن سِوى المذْكُورِينَ، ويَنْزِلُونَ مَنزِلَةَ مِن أَدَلُّوا بِهِ.

٤٨٠ . ومَن لا وارِثَ لَهُ فمالُهُ لبيت المال، يصرف في المصالح العامة والخاصة.

٤٨١ . وإذا مات الإنسان تعلق بِتَرِكَتِهِ أربعة حقوق مرتبة:

١ . أولها: مؤن التجهيز.

٢ . ثُمَّ الدُّيُونُ المَوَثَّقَةُ والمُرْسَلَةُ مِن رَأْسِ المالِ.

٣ . ثُمَّ إذا كانَ لَهُ وصِيَّةٌ تَنْفُذُ مِن ثُلُثِهِ لِلْأَجْنَبِيِّ.

٤ . ثُمَّ الباقِي لِلْوَرَثَةِ المذْكُورِينَ، واللَّهُ أَعْلَمُ.

**482.** The means of inheritance are:

1.  Lineage
2.  A valid marriage
3.  Patronage due to manumission

**483.** The impediments of inheritance are:

1.  Murder
2.  Slavery
3.  Difference of religion

**484.** If any of the heirs are foetuses or are missing, then caution is to be observed, and their share is held for them. If the heirs demand the distribution of the inheritance, then necessary precaution is to be taken according to what the jurists, may Allāh ﷻ have mercy on them, have decided.

٤٨٢. وأسْبابُ الإِرْثِ ثَلاثَةٌ:

١. النَّسَبُ

٢. والنِّكاحُ الصَّحيحُ

٣. والولاء

٤٨٣. وموانعه ثلاثة:

١. القتل

٢. والرق،

٣. واختلاف الدين.

٤٨٤. وإذا كانَ بَعْضُ الوَرَثَةِ حَمْلًا أَوْ مَفْقُودًا أَوْ نَحْوَهُ:
عَمِلْتَ بِالاحْتِياطِ وَوَقَفْتَ لَهُ، إِنْ طَلَبَ الوَرَثَةُ قِسْمَةَ الميراثِ
عَمِلْتَ ما يَحْصُلُ بِهِ الاحْتِياطُ عَلى حَسَبِ ما قَرَّرَهُ
الفُقَهاءُ، رحمهم الله تعالى.

# بَابُ العِتْق

# Chapter: Manumission of Slaves

485. ʿItq is defined as the freeing of slaves from the shackles of slavery.

486. It is considered to be from the best acts of worship as per the *ḥadīth*, "Whoever frees a Muslim slave, Allāh ﷻ will save all the parts of his body from the Hellfire just as he has freed the body-parts of the slave." (Agreed upon)

487. The Prophet ﷺ was asked what type of manumission was best, to which he ﷺ replied, "The one who is most valuable in price and most precious to his master." (Agreed upon)

488. It occurs by the following:

1. Verbally stating it by stating the term ʿitq (manumission) or something that is synonymous in meaning.

2. By ownership. Thus, whoever possesses a *maḥram* relative through blood ties becomes free.

3. Mutilation. If a slave owner cuts off a limb or burns it, the slave will be set free.

# بابُ العِتْقِ

٤٨٥. وهُوَ تَحْرِيرُ الرَّقَبَةِ وتَخْليصُها مِن الرِّق.

٤٨٦. وهو من أفضل العبادات؛ لحديث: «أيّما امرئ مسلم أعتق امرأً مسلمًا استنقذ الله بكل عضو منه عضوًا منه من النار» مُتَّفَقٌ عَلَيْهِ.

٤٨٧. وسُئِلَ رَسُولُ اللهِ ﷺ: «أيُّ الرِّقابِ أفضلُ؟ فَقالَ: «أغْلاها ثَمَنًا، وأنْفَسُها عِنْدَ أهْلِها» مُتَّفَقٌ عَلَيْهِ.

٤٨٨. ويَحْصُلُ العِتْقُ:

١. بِالقَوْلِ: وهُوَ لَفْظُ العِتْقِ وما فِي مَعْناهُ.

٢. وبالمِلك، فَمَن مَلَكَ ذا رحمٍ مُحَرَّمٍ مِن النَّسَبِ عَتَقَ عَلَيْهِ.

٣. وبِالتَّمْثِيلِ بِعَبْدِهِ بِقَطْعِ عُضْوٍ مِن أعْضائِهِ أوْ تحريقه.

4. Partial manumission, as per the *ḥadīth*, "Whoever frees his share of a common slave, and has sufficient money to free him completely, should let its price be estimated by a just man. [He should] give his partners the price of their shares and free the slave, otherwise (i.e. if he has not sufficient money) he frees the slave partially." Another version of the *ḥadīth* states, "... and if he does not have sufficient money to free him, then the price of the slave should be estimated justly, and he is to be allowed to work and earn the amount that will free him [without overburdening him]." (Agreed upon)

**489.** If the master makes manumission conditional upon the his own death, the slave is called *mudabbar.* He will be set free upon the master's death if his freedom is covered by up to one third of the master's estate. It was narrated on the authority of Jābir ﷺ that a man from the Anṣār declared that his young slave boy would become free after his death, yet he had no other property. When the Prophet ﷺ heard of this he said, "Who will buy this slave from me?" So Nuʿaym bin Abdullāh ﷺ bought him for 800 *dirhams* even though he was in debt. The Prophet ﷺ then said, "Pay off your debt." (Agreed upon)

**490.** *Kitābah* is when a slave buys himself (i.e. his freedom) from his master with a deferred payment in two or more instalments.

٤ . وبِالسّرايةِ؛ لِحَدِيثٍ: «مَن أعْتَقَ شِرْكًا لَهُ في عَبْدٍ فَكانَ لَهُ مالٌ يَبْلُغُ ثَمَنَ العبد قُوِّم عليه قيمة عدل، فأُعطي شُرَكاؤُهُ حِصَصَهُمْ وعَتَقَ عَلَيْهِ العَبْدُ، وإلّا فقد عتق ما عليه ما عَتَقَ» وفي لَفْظٍ: «وإلّا قُوِّم عَلَيْهِ، واستُسْعِيَ غَيْرَ مَشْقُوقٍ عَلَيْهِ.» مُتَّفَق عَلَيْه

٤٨٩ . فَإِنْ عَلَّقَ عِتْقَهُ بِمَوْتِهِ فَهُوَ المدَبَّر، يُعْتَقُ بِمَوْتِهِ إذا خَرَجَ مِن الثُّلُثِ؛ فَعَنْ جابِرٍ: أنَّ رجُلًا مِن الأنْصارِ أعْتَقَ غُلامًا لَهُ عَنْ دُبُرٍ لَمْ يَكُنْ لَهُ مالٌ غَيْرُهُ، فَبَلَغَ ذَلِكَ النَّبِيَّ ﷺ فَقالَ: «مَن يَشْتَرِيهِ مِنّي»؟ فاشْتَراهُ نَعِيمُ بْنُ عَبْدِ اللهِ بِثَمانِمائَة دِرْهَمٍ، وكانَ عَلَيْهِ دَيْنٌ فَأعْطاهُ، وقالَ: «اقضِ دَيْنَكَ» مُتَّفَقٌ عَلَيْه

٤٩٠ . والكِتابَةِ: أنْ يَشْتَرِيَ الرَّقِيقَ نَفْسَهُ مِن سَيِّدِهِ بِثَمَنٍ مُؤَجَّلٍ بِأجَلَيْنِ فَأكْثَر.

**491.** Allāh ﷻ says: *"...If any of your slaves wish to pay for their freedom, make a contract with them accordingly if you know they have good in them, and give them some of the wealth God has given you."* (24: 33) In other words, [make the contract] if they are righteous and have the ability to earn a living.

**492.** However, if it is feared that he will fall into evil by his manumission or *kitābah,* or if he does not have the means to earn a living, it is not allowed to manumit him or offer him freedom in return for a price.

**493.** A *mukātab* (a slave who entered into an agreement to buy his freedom) is not to be manumitted except by fulfilment of the agreement as per the *ḥadīth,* "The *mukātab* is a slave as long as a dirham of the agreed price remains to be paid." (Abū Dāwūd)

**494.** Ibn ʿAbbās ﷺ narrated in a *marfūʿ* form, and ʿUmar ﷺ narrated in a *mawqūf* form, that, "When a man's female slave bears him a child, she becomes free when he dies." (Ibn Mājah). It seems as though it is more accurate to say that this is a statement of ʿUmar ﷺ.

And Allāh ﷻ knows best.

٤٩١. قالَ تَعالى: ﴿وَالَّذِينَ يَبْتَغُونَ الْكِتَبَ مِمَّا مَلَكَتْ أَيْمَنُكُمْ فَكَاتِبُوهُمْ إِنْ عَلِمْتُمْ فِيهِمْ خَيْرًا﴾ [النُّورِ:٣٣]

يَعْنِي: صَلاحًا فِي دِينِهِمْ وَكَسْبًا.

٤٩٢. فَإِنْ خِيفَ مِنهُ الفَسادُ بِعِتْقِهِ أَوْ كِتابَتِهِ، أَوْ لَيْسَ لَهُ كَسَبَ، فَلا يُشْرَعُ عتقه ولا كتابته.

٤٩٣. ولا يعتق المكاتب إلا بالأداء؛ لحديث: «المكاتب عبد ما بقي عليه من كتابته درهم» رَواهُ أَبُو داؤدَ.

٤٩٤. وعَنِ ابْنِ عَبّاسٍ مَرْفُوعًا، وعَنْ عُمَرَ موقوفًا: «أَيُّما أمةٍ ولَدَتْ مِن سَيِّدِها فَهِيَ حُرَّةٌ بَعْدَ مَوْتِهِ» أَخْرَجَهُ ابْنُ ماجَه، والرّاجِحُ المَوْقُوفُ عَلى عُمَرَ رضي الله عنه.


والله أعلم

115

# كِتَابُ النِّكَاح

# The Book of Marriage

**495.** Marriage is from the way of the Messengers.

**496.** The Prophet ﷺ said, "O young people! Whoever amongst you is able to marry should marry, for it helps in lowering one's gaze and guarding one's private parts; and whoever is not able to marry should fast, as fasting diminishes one's sexual desires." (Agreed upon)

**497.** He ﷺ also said, "A woman is married for four reasons: her wealth, status, beauty, and religion. Choose the one who is religious, may your hands be rubbed with dust (i.e. may you prosper)." (Agreed upon)

**498.** One should choose someone who is religious, has status, is loving, and is fertile.

**499.** If one desires to propose to a woman, he may look at whatever encourages him to marry her.

**500.** It is not permissible to propose to a woman who has already been proposed to by another Muslim unless the latter permits him or leaves the matter.

# كِتابُ النِّكاحِ

٤٩٥. وهُوَ مِن سُنَنِ المرْسَلِينَ.

٤٩٦. وفِي الحَدِيثِ: «يا مَعْشَرَ الشَّبابِ، مَن اسْتَطاعَ مِنكُم الباءةَ فَلْيَتَزَوَّجْ، فإنَّهُ أغَضُّ لِلْبَصَرِ وأحْصَنُ لِلْفَرْجِ، ومَن لَمْ يَسْتَطِعْ فعَلَيْهِ بِالصَّوْمِ، فإنَّهُ لَهُ وجاءٌ» مُتَّفقٌ عَلَيْهِ.

٤٩٧. وقالَ ﷺ: «تُنْكَحُ المرْأةُ لأرْبَعٍ: لِمالِها، وحَسَبِها، وجَمالِها، ودِينِها، فاظْفَرْ بِذاتِ الدِّينِ تَرِبَتْ يَمِينُكَ» مُتَّفَقٌ عَلَيْهِ.

٤٩٨. ويَنْبَغِي أنْ يَتَنَخَّيَّرَ ذاتَ الدِّينِ والحَسَبِ، الوَدُودَ الولود الحسيبة.

٤٩٩. وإذا وقع في قلبه خطبة امرأة فله أن ينظر منها ما يدعوه إلى نكاحها.

٥٠٠. ولا يَحِلُّ لِلرَّجُلِ أنْ يَخْطُبَ عَلى خِطْبَةِ أخِيهِ المسْلِمِ، حَتَّى يَأْذَنَ أوْ يَتْرُكَ.

**501.** It is not allowed to explicitly propose to the *muʿtaddah* (a woman in her waiting period).

**502.** It is permissible to implicitly propose to a *bāʾin* (irrevocably divorced woman or widow) as per the statement of Allāh ﷻ *"You will not be blamed if you hint that you wish to marry these women, or keep it to yourselves - God knows that you intend to propose to them..."* (2:235)

**503.** The way to allude to one's desire to propose is to say, for example, "I am interested in someone like you" or "do not let me miss an opportunity [to marry you]" and so on.

**504.** One should read the sermon of Ibn Masʿūd ﷺ during the contract of marriage. He said, "The Prophet ﷺ taught us the sermon for times of need: 'Praise be to Allāh ﷻ from Whom we ask help and pardon, and in Whom we take refuge from the evils within ourselves. He whom Allāh ﷻ guides has no one who can lead him astray, and he whom He leads astray has no one to guide him. I testify that there is no god but Allāh ﷻ, and I testify that Muḥammad ﷺ is His servant and Messenger.' He should then read the three verses." (Reported by the narrators of the *sunan*.) The three verses were explained by some to be:

٥٠١. وَلَا يَجُوزُ التَّصْرِيحُ بِخِطْبَةِ المُعْتَدَّةِ مُطْلَقًا.

٥٠٢. وَيَجُوزُ التَّعْرِيضُ فِي خِطْبَةِ البَائِنِ بِمَوْتٍ أَوْ غَيْرِهِ؛ لِقَوْلِهِ تَعَالَى: ﴿وَلَا جُنَاحَ عَلَيْكُمْ فِيمَا عَرَّضْتُم بِهِۦ مِنْ خِطْبَةِ ٱلنِّسَآءِ﴾ [البَقَرَة: ٢٣٥]

٥٠٣. وَصِفَةُ التَّعْرِيضِ، أَنْ يَقُولَ: إِنِّي فِي مِثْلِكِ لَرَاغِبٌ، أَوْ لَا تُفَوِّتِينِي نَفْسَكِ، وَنَحْوَهَا.

٥٠٤. وَيَنْبَغِي أَنْ يَخْطُبَ فِي عَقْدِ النِّكَاحِ بِخُطْبَةِ ابْنِ مَسْعُودٍ، قَالَ: عَلَّمَنَا رَسُولُ اللهِ ﷺ التَّشَهُّدَ فِي الحَاجَةِ: إِنَّ الحَمْدَ لِلَّهِ، نَحْمَدُهُ، وَنَسْتَعِينُهُ، وَنَسْتَغْفِرُهُ، وَنَعُوذُ بِاللهِ مِنْ شُرُورِ أَنْفُسِنَا وَسَيِّئَاتِ أَعْمَالِنَا، مَنْ يَهْدِهِ اللهُ فَلَا مُضِلَّ لَهُ، وَمَن يَضْلِل فَلَا هَادِي لَه، وَأَشْهَد أَن لَا إِله إِلَّا الله، وَحْدَهُ لَا شَرِيكَ لَهُ، وَأَشْهَدُ أَنَّ مُحَمَّدًا عبده وَرَسُولُهُ، وَيَقْرَأُ ثَلَاثَ آيَاتٍ» رَوَاهُ أَهْلُ السُّنَنِ، وَالثَّلَاثُ الآيَاتِ فَسَّرَهَا بَعْضُهُمْ، وَهِيَ:

*"O You who believe, be mindful of God, as is His due, and make sure you devote yourselves to Him until your dying moment."* (3:102)

*"O People, be mindful of your Lord Who created you from a single soul, and from it created its mate, and from the pair of them spread countless men and women far and wide; be mindful of God, in Whose name you make requests of one another. Beware of severing the ties of kinship: God is always watching over you."* (4:1)

*"O you who believe, be mindful of God, speak in a direct fashion and to good purpose, and He will put your deeds right for you and forgive you your sins. Whoever obeys God and His Messenger will truly achieve a great triumph."* (33: 70-71)

**505.** Marriage comes into effect by:

1. An offer: this is by a verbal statement from the guardian such as: *zawwajtuka* (I marry you to her) or *ankaḥtuka.*
2. Acceptance: this is by a verbal statement from the husband or his representative such as: *qabiltu hadha al-zawāj* (I accept this marriage) or *qabiltu* (I accept), and so on.

١. قَوْلُهُ تَعالى: ﴿يَـٰٓأَيُّهَا ٱلَّذِينَ ءَامَنُوا۟ ٱتَّقُوا۟ ٱللَّهَ حَقَّ تُقَاتِهِۦ وَلَا تَمُوتُنَّ إِلَّا وَأَنتُم مُّسْلِمُونَ﴾ [آل عمران: ١٠٢]

٢. وَالآيَةُ الأُولَى مِن سُورَةِ النِّساءِ: ﴿يَـٰٓأَيُّهَا ٱلنَّاسُ ٱتَّقُوا۟ رَبَّكُمُ ٱلَّذِى خَلَقَكُم مِّن نَّفْسٍ وَٰحِدَةٍ وَخَلَقَ مِنْهَا زَوْجَهَا وَبَثَّ مِنْهُمَا رِجَالًا كَثِيرًا وَنِسَآءً وَٱتَّقُوا۟ ٱللَّهَ ٱلَّذِى تَسَآءَلُونَ بِهِۦ وَٱلْأَرْحَامَ إِنَّ ٱللَّهَ كَانَ عَلَيْكُمْ رَقِيبًا ۝﴾ [النساء: ۝]

٣. وقَوْلُهُ تَعال: ﴿يَـٰٓأَيُّهَا ٱلَّذِينَ ءَامَنُوا۟ ٱتَّقُوا۟ ٱللَّهَ وَقُولُوا۟ قَوْلًا سَدِيدًا ۝ يُصْلِحْ لَكُمْ أَعْمَٰلَكُمْ وَيَغْفِرْ لَكُمْ ذُنُوبَكُمْ وَمَن يُطِعِ ٱللَّهَ وَرَسُولَهُۥ فَقَدْ فَازَ فَوْزًا عَظِيمًا ۝﴾ [الأحزاب: ٧٠-٧١]

٥٠٥. ولا يجب إلا:

١. بِالإِيجَابِ: وهُوَ اللَّفْظُ الصّادِرُ مِن الوَلِيّ، كقوله: زَوَّجْتُك، أو أَنْكَحْتُك.

٢. والقَبُول: وهُوَ اللَّفْظُ الصّادِرُ مِن الزَّوْجِ أُوْ نائِبِهِ، كَقَوْلِهِ: قَبِلْتُ هَذا الزَّواجَ، أُوْ قبِلت، ونحوه.

121

# بَابُ شُرُوطِ النِّكَاح

# Chapter: Conditions for Marriage

**506.** Both marriage partners must agree to the marriage except:

1. A minor, for her father can compel her.
2. A female slave, for her master can compel her.

**507.** A woman must have a *wali* (guardian). The Prophet ﷺ said, "A marriage is not acceptable except with a guardian." (Aḥmad, Abū Dāwūd, and others)

**508.** The most entitled to marry off a free woman is:

1. Her father and then his ascendants.
2. Then her son and then his descendants.
3. Then those closet in paternal relations.

**509.** The Prophet ﷺ said, "A matron should not be given in marriage except after consulting her; and a virgin should not be given in marriage except after her permission." The people asked, "O Messenger of Allāh! How can we know her permission?" He ﷺ said, "her silence [indicates her permission]." (Agreed upon)

# بابُ شُرُوطِ النِّكاحِ

٥٠٦. ولابد فِيهِ مِن رِضا الزَّوْجَيْنِ إلّا:

١. الصَّغِيرَةُ فيجبرها أبوها.

٢. والأمة يجبرها سيدها.

٥٠٧. ولابد فيه من الولي؛ قال ﷺ: «لا نِكاحَ إلا بِوَلِيٍّ» حديث صحيح، رواه الخمسة.

٥٠٨. وأوْلى النّاسِ بِتَزْوِيج الحُرَّةِ:

١. أبُوها وإنْ عَلا.

٢. ثُمَّ اِبْنُها وإنْ نَزَلَ.

٣. ثُمَّ الأقْرَبُ فالأقْرَبُ مِن عَصَباتِها.

٥٠٩. وفِي الحَدِيثِ المُتَّفَقِ عَلَيْهِ: «لا تُنْكَحُ الأيِّمُ حَتّى تُسْتأْمَر، ولا تُنْكَحُ البِكْرُ حَتّى تُسْتأْذَنَ»، قالُوا: يا رَسُولَ اللهِ، وكَيْفَ إذْنُها؟ قال: «أنْ تَسْكُتَ»

123

**510.** The Prophet ﷺ said, "Announce the marriage." (Aḥmad)

Announcing the marriage incorporates having two just witnesses, openly declaring it, and using the *duff* or equivalent.

**511.** The guardian does not have the right to marry her to someone who is not *kufʾ* (suitable) for her. Thus, the evildoer is not suitable for a chaste woman. Arabs are suitable for one another, and so on.

**512.** If the guardian is missing or has disappeared for a long period of time or prevents her from marrying someone suitable for her, the ruler has the right to marry her off as mentioned in the *ḥadīth*, "The leader is the guardian for the one who has no guardian." (Reported in the *sunan* except al-Nasāʾī)

**513.** It is imperative to explicitly specify the bride. Thus, to say, "I have married you to *my daughter*" whilst he has other daughters is not correct until he specifies her by name or description.

**514.** It is also necessary for there not to be any impediments to the marriage. These matters are mentioned in the [following] chapter, "Those Who are Prohibited to Marry".

٥١٠. وقالَ النَّبيُّ ﷺ: «أَعْلِنُوا النِّكاحَ» رواه أحمد. ومن إعلانه: شهادة عدلين، وإشهاره وإظهاره، والضرب عليه بالدف، ونحوه.

٥١١. ولَيْسَ لِوَليِّ المرأةِ تَزْويجُها بِغَيْرِ كفءٍ لَها، فليس الفاجر كفؤًا لِلْعَفيفةِ. والعَرَبُ بَعْضُهُمْ لِبَعْضٍ أكْفاء.

٥١٢. فإنْ عُدِمَ وليُّها، أو غابَ غِيبةً طَويلَةً، أو امْتَنَعَ مِن تَزْويجِها كُفْؤًا: زَوَّجَها الحاكِمُ، كَما في الحَديثِ: «السُّلْطانُ وليُّ مَن لا وليَّ لَهُ» أخرجه أصحاب السنن إلا النسائي.

٥١٣. ولابد مِن تَعْيينِ مَن يَقَعُ عَلَيْهِ العَقْدُ، فَلا يَصِحُّ: زَوَّجْتُكَ بِنْتي ولَهُ غَيْرُها، حَتّى يُمَيِّزَها باسمها أو وصفها.

٥١٤. ولابد أيْضًا مِن عَدَمِ الموانِعِ بأحَدِ الزَّوْجَيْنِ، وهِيَ المذكورة في باب المحرمات في النكاح.

# بَابُ المُحَرَّمَات في النِّكَاح

# Chapter: Those Who Are Prohibited to Marry

515. Women that are prohibited to marry are of two types:

1. Those who are permanently prohibited.
2. Those who are temporarily prohibited.

516. Those who are permanently prohibited to marry are:

A. Seven due to kinship, who are:

1. Mothers and their ascendants.
2. Daughters and their descendants. This includes the daughters of one's daughter.
3. Sisters.
4. Their daughters.
5. The brother's daughters.
6. Paternal aunties.
7. Maternal aunties. These include the aunties of his ascendants (i.e. his father's aunties, grandfather's or mother's, and so on.)

# بابُ المُحَرَّماتِ في النِّكاحِ

٥١٥. وهن قسمان:

١. مُحَرَّماتٌ إلى الأبدِ.

٢. ومُحَرَّماتٌ إلى أَمَدٍ.

٥١٦. فالمُحَرَّماتُ إلى الأبدِ:

أ. سَبْعٌ مِنَ النَّسَبِ، وهُنَّ:

١ –الأُمَّهاتُ وإنْ عَلَوْنَ.

٢ –والبَناتُ وإنْ نَزَلْنَ، ولَوْ مِن بَناتِ البِنْتِ.

٣ –والأَخَواتُ مُطْلَقًا.

٤ –وبناتهن.

٥ –وبنات الإخوة.

٦، ٧. والعمات، والخالات، له أو لأحد أصوله.

B. Seven due to suckling: They correspond to the above.
C. Four due to relationships by marriage:
   1. The wives' mothers and their ascendants.
   2. The wives' daughters and their descendants if the husband consummated the marriage with the mothers.
   3. The fathers' wives and their ascendants.
   4. The sons' wives and their descendants by lineage or suckling.

**517.** This is based upon the saying of Allāh ﷻ:

*"You are forbidden to take as wives your mothers, daughters, sisters, paternal and maternal aunts, the daughters of brothers and daughters of sisters, your milk-mothers and milk-sisters, your wives' mothers, the stepdaughters in your care - those born of women with whom you have consummated marriage, if you have not consummated the marriage, then you will not be blamed - wives of your begotten sons, two sisters simultaneously - with the exception of what has passed: God is most forgiving and merciful – and women already married, other than your slaves. God has ordained all this for you. Other women are lawful to you, so long as you seek them in marriage, with gifts from your property, looking for wedlock rather than fornication. If you wish to enjoy women through marriage, give them their bride-gift - this is obligatory - though if you should choose mutually, after fulfilling this obligation, to do otherwise [with the bride-gift], you will not be blamed: God is all knowing and all wise."* (4:23-24)

ب. وسبع من الرضاع، نظير المذكورات.

ج. وأربع من الصِّهر، وهن:

١. أُمَّهاتُ الزَّوجاتِ، وإنْ عَلَوْنَ،

٢. وبَناتُهُنَّ، وإنْ نَزَلْنَ، إذا كانَ قَدْ دَخَلَ بِأُمَّهاتِهِنَّ.

٣. وزَوْجاتُ الآباءِ، وإنْ عَلَوْنَ.

٤. وزَوْجاتُ الأبناءِ، وإنْ نَزَلْنَ،

مِن نَسَبٍ أوْ رَضاعَ.

٥١٧. والأصلُ في هَذا قَوْلُهُ تَعالى: ﴿حُرِّمَتْ عَلَيْكُمْ أُمَّهَٰتُكُمْ وَبَنَاتُكُمْ وَأَخَوَٰتُكُمْ وَعَمَّٰتُكُمْ وَخَٰلَٰتُكُمْ وَبَنَاتُ ٱلْأَخِ وَبَنَاتُ ٱلْأُخْتِ وَأُمَّهَٰتُكُمُ ٱلَّٰتِي أَرْضَعْنَكُمْ وَأَخَوَٰتُكُم مِّنَ ٱلرَّضَٰعَةِ وَأُمَّهَٰتُ نِسَآئِكُمْ وَرَبَٰٓئِبُكُمُ ٱلَّٰتِي فِي حُجُورِكُم مِّن نِّسَآئِكُمُ ٱلَّٰتِي دَخَلْتُم بِهِنَّ فَإِن لَّمْ تَكُونُواْ دَخَلْتُم بِهِنَّ فَلَا جُنَاحَ عَلَيْكُمْ وَحَلَٰٓئِلُ أَبْنَآئِكُمُ ٱلَّذِينَ مِنْ أَصْلَٰبِكُمْ وَأَن تَجْمَعُواْ بَيْنَ ٱلْأُخْتَيْنِ إِلَّا مَا قَدْ سَلَفَ إِنَّ ٱللَّهَ كَانَ غَفُورًا رَّحِيمًا﴾ [النساء:٢٣]

[It is also based on] the *ḥadīth*, "That which is prohibited due to lineage or childbirth relations is also prohibited through suckling." (Agreed upon)

518. Those who are temporarily prohibited to marry are:

1. Those mentioned in the *ḥadīth*, "A man cannot marry both a woman and her paternal or maternal auntie at the same time." (Agreed upon)
2. Those mentioned in the verse, "*... and two sisters in wedlock at the same time.*" (4:23)

519. It is not allowed for a free man to marry more than four women at any one time, and a slave is not allowed to marry more than two at a time.

520. However, he has the right to have intercourse with what his right hand possesses (i.e. slaves).

521. If a disbeliever embraces *Islām* and has two wives who are sisters, he has to choose one of the two and separate from the other. Likewise, if he has more than four wives, he has to choose four and separate from the others.

قَوْلُهُ ﷺ: «يَحْرُمُ مِنَ الرَّضاعِ ما يَحْرُمُ مِنَ النَّسَبِ أو مِنَ الوِلادَةِ» مُتَّفَق عَلَيْهِ.

٥١٨. وأمّا المُحَرَّماتُ إلى أَمَدٍ:

١. فَمِنهُنَّ قَوْلُهُ ﷺ: «لا يُجْمَعُ بَيْنَ المرأةِ وعَمَّتِها، ولا بَيْنَ المرأةِ وخالَتِها» متفق عليه.

٢. مَعَ قَوْلِهِ تَعالى: ﴿وأَنْ تَجْمَعُوا بَيْنَ الأُخْتَيْنِ﴾ [النساء:٢٣]

٥١٩. ولا يَجُوزُ لِلْحُرِّ أَنْ يَجْمَعَ أَكْثَرَ مِن أَرْبَعٍ، ولا لِلْعَبْدِ أَنْ يَجْمَعَ أَكْثَرَ مِن زَوْجَتَيْنِ.

٥٢٠. وأمّا مِلْكُ اليَمِينِ، فَلَهُ أَنْ يَطَأَ ما شاءَ.

٥٢١. وإذا أسْلَمَ الكافِرُ وتَحْتَهُ أُخْتانِ، اِخْتارَ إحْداهُما، أَوْ عِنْدَهُ أَكْثَرُ مِن أَرْبَعِ زَوْجاتٍ، اِخْتارَ أَرْبَعًا، وفارَقَ البَواقِيَ.

131

**522.** It is prohibited to marry:

1. A woman in the state of *iḥrām* (inviolability) until she leaves it.
2. A *muʿtaddah* (a woman in her waiting period after divorce or due to the death of her husband) until the decreed period reaches its end.
3. A fornicator until she repents.
4. A woman who has been divorced three times until she marries another husband, consummates the marriage, and then is divorced and has finished her waiting period.

**523.** It is permissible to own two sisters, but if he had intercourse with one of them, the other sister will not be permissible for him [for intercourse] until he makes the other sister impermissible for him by no longer possessing her, or by marrying her off to somebody else after *istibrāʾ* (ascertaining that she is not pregnant).

**524.** Breastfeeding that prohibits marriage is only that which was done before weaning.

**525.** Another condition is that [the breastfeeding] must have been at least five separate feeds.

٥٢٢. وتَحْرُم:

١. المُحرِمَة حتى تحل من إحرامها.

٢. والمعتدة من الغير حتى يبلغ الكتاب أجله.

٣. والزانية على الزاني وغيره حتى تتوب.

٤. وتَحْرُمُ مُطَلَّقَتُهُ ثَلاثًا حَتَّى تَنْكِحَ زَوْجًا غَيْرُهُ، ويَطَؤُها ويُفارِقُها، وتَنْقَضِيَ عِدَّتُها.

٥٢٣. ويَجُوزُ الجَمْعُ بَيْنَ الأُخْتَيْنِ بالمِلْكِ، ولَكِنْ إذا وَطِئَ إِحْداهُما لَمْ تَحِلْ لَهُ الأُخْرى حَتَّى يُحَرِّمَ المَوْطُوءَةَ بإخْراجٍ عَنْ مِلْكِهِ، أوْ تَزَوُّجٍ لَهَا بَعْدَ الاسْتِبْراءِ.

٥٢٤. والرَّضاعُ الذِي يُحَرِّمُ، ما كانَ قَبْلَ الفِطامِ.

٥٢٥. وهُوَ خَمْسُ رَضَعاتٍ فأكْثِرُ

526. The child and their [future] children will be considered as foster children to the wet nurse and her husband.

527. The impermissibility of marriage is also established through the wet nurse and her husband just as it is through lineage.

٥٢٦. فَيَصِيرُ بِهِ الطِّفْلُ وأَوْلادُهُ أَوْلادًا لِلْمُرْضِعَةِ وصاحِبِ اللَّبَنِ.

٥٢٧. ويَنْتَشِرُ التَّحْرِيمُ مِن جِهَةِ المُرْضِعَةِ وصاحِبِ اللَّبَنِ كانْتِشارِ النَّسَبِ.

# بَابُ الشُّرُوطِ في النِّكَاح

# Chapter: Conditions within the Marriage Contract

**528.** These are conditions stipulated by either spouse upon the other.

**529.** They are of two types:

1. Valid: such as stipulating that he is not allowed to have another wife, or that he is not allowed to have concubines, or that he is not allowed move her to another house or another country, or to have an increase in the dowry or in expenditure, and so on. This all falls under the statement of the Prophet ﷺ "The conditions that are most deserving of fulfilment are those by means sexual intercourse becomes allowed to you." (Agreed upon)

2. Invalid conditions: such as *mutʿah* (temporary marriage), *taḥlīl* (marriage with the intention to divorce to facilitate the remarriage of a divorced couple), and *shighār* (marrying one's daughter to man with the condition that he can marry the man's daughter in lieu of any dowry between the two.)

# بابُ الشُّروطِ في النِّكاحِ

٥٢٨. وهِيَ ما يَشْتَرِطُهُ أحَدُ الزَّوْجَيْنِ عَلى الآخَرِ.

٥٢٩. وهِيَ قِسْمانِ:

١. صَحِيحٌ، كاشْتِراطِ أنْ لا يَتَزَوَّجَ عليها، أو لا يَتَسَرّى، ولا يُخْرِجَها مِن دارِها، أو بَلَدِها، أوْ زِيادَةِ مهرٍ أوْ نفقةٍ، ونَحْوِ ذَلِكَ، فَهَذا ونَحْوُهُ كُلُّهُ داخِلٌ في قَوْلِهِ ﷺ: «إنَّ أحَقَّ الشُّروطِ أنْ تُوَفُّوا بِهِ، ما اسْتَحْلَلْتُمْ بِهِ الفُروجَ» مُتَّفَقٌ عَلَيْهِ.

٢. ومِنها شُروطٌ فاسِدَةٌ، كَنِكاحِ المُتْعَةِ، والتَّحْلِيلِ والشِّغارِ.

- "The Prophet ﷺ initially allowed *mutʿah* then prohibited it thereafter." (Muslim)
- "He ﷺ also cursed the *muḥallil* (the one who practices *taḥlīl*) and the *muḥallal lahu* (the one for whom *taḥlīl* was done).
- He ﷺ also forbade the practice of *shighār*.

These are all authentic narrations.

- «ورخَّص النَّبِيُّ ﷺ في المتْعَةِ أوَّلًا، ثُمَّ حَرَّمَها.»

- «ولَعَنَ المَحَلِّلَ والمَحَلَّلَ لَهُ.»

- «ونَهى عَنْ نِكاحِ الشِّغارِ وهُوَ: أنْ يُزَوِّجَهُ مُوَلِّيَتَهُ عَلى أنْ يُزَوِّجَهُ الآخَرُ مُوَلِّيَتَهُ، ولا مَهْرَ بَيْنَهُما.»


وكُلُّها أحادِيثُ صَحِيحَةٌ.

# بَابُ العُيُوب في النِّكَاح

# Chapter: Defects in Spouses

530. If a spouse finds a defect in their partner that he/she was unaware of before the marriage contract such as insanity and leprosy etc, they have a right to annul the marriage.

531. If the wife found her husband to be impotent, he should be given respite for a year. If he still remains impotent after a year, she has the right to annul the marriage.

532. If a wife was emancipated from slavery whilst her husband remained a slave, she has the choice to either remain with him or leave him as per the long ḥadīth regarding the story of Barīrah, where "...she was given the choice regarding her husband after she was emancipated." (Agreed upon)

533. If the marriage is annulled before consummation, no dowry needs to be given to the wife.

534. However, after consummation, the dowry becomes due, and the husband may seek a reimbursement from the one who deceived him.

# بابُ العُيُوبِ في النّكاحِ

٥٣٠. إذا وجَدَ أحدُ الزّوْجَيْنِ بالآخَرِ عَيْبًا لَمْ يَعْلَمْ بِهِ قَبْلَ العَقْدِ، كالجُنُونِ والجُذامِ والبَرَصِ ونَحْوِها، فَلَهُ فَسْخُ النكاح.

٥٣١. وإذا وجدته عِنِّينًا: أُجِّلَ إلى سَنَةٍ، فإنْ مَضَتْ وهُوَ عَلى حاله فلها الفسخ.

٥٣٢. وإذا عتقت كلها وزوْجُها رَقيقٌ، خُيِّرَتْ بَيْنَ المقامِ مَعَهُ وفِراقِه؛ لحديث عائشة الطويل في قصة بَرِيَرة: «خُيِّرَتْ بَرِيَرَةُ عَلى زوْجِها حِينَ عَتَقَتْ». مُتَّفَقٌ عليه.

٥٣٣. وإذا وقَعَ الفَسْخُ قَبْلَ الدُّخُولِ فَلا مَهْرَ.

٥٣٤. وبَعْدَهُ يَسْتَقِرُّ، ويَرْجِعُ الزّوْجُ عَلى مَن غَرَّهُ.

# كِتَابُ الصَّدَاق

# The Book of Dowries

**535.** It is appropriate to make it moderate in amount.

ʿĀʾishah ﷺ was asked, "How much was the dowry of the Prophet ﷺ?" To which she replied, "His dowry for his wives was 12 *ūqiyyah* and a *nash*. Do you know what a *nash* is?" She said "no" to which she replied, "It is half an *ūqiyyah*. So that is a total of 500 *dirham*." (Muslim)

**536.** The Prophet ﷺ emancipated Ṣafiyyah ﷺ and made her emancipation her dowry. (Agreed upon)

**537.** He ﷺ said to a man, "Look for something to give, even if is an iron ring." (Agreed upon) Thus, anything considered to have value, even if insignificant in amount, is acceptable to give as dowry.

**538.** If a man marries a woman without specifying her dowry, she is entitled to have what most women in her position would receive.

**539.** If he divorced her before consummating the marriage, she is entitled to *mutʿah* (alimony); the wealthy according to his capability and the poor according to his capability, as per the saying of Allāh ﷻ

# كِتابُ الصَّداقِ

٥٣٥. يَنْبَغِي تَخْفِيفُهُ

وسُئِلَتْ عائِشَةُ، كَمْ كانَ صَداقُ النَّبِيِّ ﷺ؟ قالَتْ: كانَ صَداقُهُ لِأزواجِهِ ثِنْتَي عَشْرَةَ أُوقِيَّةً ونَشّا، أَتَدْرِي ما النَّشُّ؟ قُلْتُ: لا، قالَتْ: نِصْفُ أُوقِيَّةٍ، فَتِلْكَ خَمْسُمائة دِرْهَمٍ. رَواهُ مُسْلِمٌ.

٥٣٦. وأَعْتَقَ صَفِيَّةَ وجَعَلَ عِتْقَها صَداقَها. مُتَّفَقٌ عَلَيْهِ.

٥٣٧. وقالَ لِرَجُلٍ: «التَمِسْ ولَو خاتَمًا مِن حَدِيدٍ». مُتَّفَقٌ عَلَيْهِ، فَكُلُّ ما صَحَّ ثَمَنًا وأُجْرَةً -وإنْ قَلَّ- صَحَّ صَداقًا.

٥٣٨. فَإنْ تَزَوَّجَها ولَمْ يُسَمِّ لها صَداقًا، فلَها مهر المِثْلِ.

٥٣٩. فَإنْ طَلَّقَها قَبْلَ الدُّخُولِ، فلَها المَتْعَةُ، عَلَى الموسع قدره، وعلى المقتر قدره، لِقوله تعالى

143

*"You will not be blamed if you divorce women before consummating the marriage or allocating a bride-gift for them, but make fair provision for them; the rich according to his means and the poor according to his - this is a duty for those who do good."* (2:236)

**540.** She can claim full right to the complete dowry either by consummation of the marriage or by the death of her husband.

**541.** The dowry is halved due to every separation initiated by the husband before consummation of the marriage.

**542.** She will not be entitled to the dowry if:

1. The separation was initiated by her.
2. By annulment due to her defects.

**543.** Whoever divorces his wife should give something to her as compensation in order to comfort her, as per the verse:

*"Divorced women shall also have such maintenance, as is considered fair: this is a duty for those who are mindful of God."*
(2:241)

﴿لَّا جُنَاحَ عَلَيۡكُمۡ إِن طَلَّقۡتُمُ ٱلنِّسَآءَ مَا لَمۡ تَمَسُّوهُنَّ أَوۡ تَفۡرِضُوا۟ لَهُنَّ فَرِيضَةٗۚ وَمَتِّعُوهُنَّ عَلَى ٱلۡمُوسِعِ قَدَرُهُۥ وَعَلَى ٱلۡمُقۡتِرِ قَدَرُهُۥ مَتَٰعَۢا بِٱلۡمَعۡرُوفِۖ حَقًّا عَلَى ٱلۡمُحۡسِنِينَ﴾ [البقرة:٢٣٦]

٥٤٠. ويتقرر الصداق كاملًا بالموت أو الدخول.

٥٤١. ويتنصف بكل فرقة قبل الدخول من جهة الزوج، كطلاقه.

٥٤٢. ويسقط:

١. بِفُرقة من قِبَلِها.

٢. أو فَسْخهِ لعيبها.

٥٤٣. وينبغي لمن طلق زوجته أن يمتعها بشيء يحصل به جبر خاطرها؛ لقوله تعالى: ﴿وَلِلۡمُطَلَّقَٰتِ مَتَٰعُۢ بِٱلۡمَعۡرُوفِۖ حَقًّا عَلَى ٱلۡمُتَّقِينَ﴾ [البقرة: ٢٤١]

## بَابُ عِشْرَة النِّسَاء

# Chapter: Marital Relationships

**544.** Each spouse must treat their spouse with kindness. This includes maintaining good companionship, refraining from harming one another, and not procrastinating in fulfilling each other's rights.

**545.** It is a duty upon the wife to:

1. Fulfil her husband's intimacy requirements.
2. Not leave home or travel without his permission.
3. Bake bread, knead dough, cook, and so on.

**546.** It is a duty upon the husband to provide her with financial support and clothe her, as Allāh ﷻ says:

*"And live with them honourably."* (4:19)

The Prophet ﷺ said, "Treat women well." (Agreed upon)

He ﷺ also said, "The best of you are those best to their wives." (Tirmidhī)

# بابُ عِشْرَةِ النِّساءِ

٥٤٤. يَلْزَمُ كُلَّ واحِدٍ مِن الزَّوْجَيْنِ مُعاشَرَةُ الآخَرَ بِالمَعْرُوفِ، مِن الصُّحْبَةِ الجَمِيلَةِ، وكَفِّ الأذى، وألا يمطله بحقه.

٥٤٥. ويلزمها:

١. طاعته في الاستمتاع.

٢. وعدم الخروج والسفر إلا بإذنه.

٣. والقيام بالخبز والعجن والطبخ ونحوها.

٥٤٦. وعليه نفقتها وكسوتها بالمعروف. كما قال تعالى: ﴿وَعَاشِرُوهُنَّ بِالمَعْرُوفِ﴾ [النساء:١٩]

وفي الحديث: «اسْتَوصُوا بِالنِّساءِ خَيرًا».

وفيهِ: «خَيرُكُمْ خَيرُكُمْ لأهْلِهِ»

The Prophet ﷺ said, "If a man calls his wife to bed and she refuses, the angels will curse her until the morning." (Agreed upon)

547. The husband must be as just as he can in the following: the division of nights between his wives, maintenance, and clothing.

The Prophet ﷺ said, "Whoever has two wives and favours one [over the other in treatment] will come on the Day of Judgement with one of his sides sloping." (Abū Dāwūd)

548. Anas ﷺ reported that it is from the sunnah that if one marries a virgin while already being married to [another] woman, he should stay with her (the virgin) for seven days. Thereafter, he should divide his days equally. If someone marries a previously married woman, he should stay with her for three days, and then by [equal] turns thereafter. (Agreed upon)

549. ʿĀʾishah ﷺ reported that whenever the Messenger ﷺ wanted to go on a journey, he would draw lots to determine which of his wives would accompany him, and the one whose lot was chosen would accompany him. (Agreed upon)

550. It is permissible for a wife to forfeit her right of the division of nights, her maintenance, and clothing, with the permission of her husband.

وقالَ ﷺ: «إذا دَعا الرَّجُلُ امْرَأتَهُ إلى فِراشِهِ فَأَبَتْ أنْ تَجيءَ لَعَنَتْها الملائكةُ حَتّى تُصْبِحَ» مُتَّفَقٌ عَلَيْهِ.

٥٤٧. وعَلَيْهِ: أنْ يَعْدِلَ بَيْنَ زَوْجاتِهِ في القِسْمِ، والنَّفَقَةِ، والكِسْوَةِ، وما يَقْدِرُ عَلَيْهِ مِن العَدْلِ.

وفي الحَديثِ: «مَن كانَ لَهُ امْرَأتانِ فَمالَ إلى إحْداهُما، جاءَ يَوْمَ القِيامَةِ وشِقُّهُ مائِلٌ» متفق عليه.

٥٤٨. وعن أنس: من السنة إذا تزوج الرجل البكر على الثيب أقام عندها سبعًا، ثم قسم، وإذا تزوج الثيب، أقام عندها ثلاثًا، ثم قسم. متفق عليه.

٥٤٩. وقالَتْ عائِشَةُ: كانَ رَسُولُ اللَّهِ ﷺ إذا أرادَ سَفَرًا أقْرَعَ بَيْنَ نِسائِهِ، فَأَيَّتُهُنَّ خَرَجَ سَهْمُها خَرَجَ بِها. مُتَّفَقٌ عَلَيْهِ.

٥٥٠. وإنْ أسْقَطَتِ المَرْأةُ حَقَّها مِن القَسْمِ، أوْ مِن النَّفَقَةِ أوْ الكِسْوَةِ بِإذْنِ الزَّوْجِ، جازَ ذَلِكَ.

Sawdah bint Zamʿah 🌸 gave up her allotted day for ʿĀʾishah 🌸 and so the Prophet ﷺ used to give ʿĀʾishah 🌸 her day as well as Sawdah's 🌸. (Agreed upon)

551. If one fears discord from his wife and signs of her disobedience become apparent:

1. He should admonish her.
2. If she persists, he should not sleep in the same bed with her.
3. If she is still persistent, he should hit her lightly without injuring her.

552. However, he is prohibited from doing the above if he denied his wife her rights.

553. If separation is feared between the two, then an arbitrator should be sent from each family. Both arbitrators should be familiar with the matters related to reconciliation and separation. If they both deem reconciliation to be better, the husband and wife should stay together, with or without compensation. However, if they see separation the only option, then that is permissible.

And Allāh 🌸 knows best.

وقَدْ وهَبَتْ سَوْدَةُ بِنْتُ زَمْعَةَ يَوْمَها لِعائِشَةَ، فكانَ النَّبِيُّ ﷺ يَقْسِمُ لِعائِشَةَ يَوْمَها ويَوْمَ سَوْدَةَ. مُتَّفَقٌ عَلَيْهِ.

٥٥١. وإنْ خافَ نُشُوزَ اِمْرَأَتِهِ، وظهرت منها قرائن معصيته:

١. وعظها.

٢. فإن أصرت هجرها في المضجع.

٣. فإن لم ترتدع ضربها ضربًا غير مُبَرِّحٍ.

٥٥٢. ويمنع من ذلك إن كان مانعًا لحقها.

٥٥٣. وإن خيف الشقاق بينهما، بعث الحاكم حكمًا من أهله وحكمًا من أهلها يعرفان الأمور والجمع والتفريق، يجمعان إن رأيا بعوض أو غيره، أو يفرقان، فما فعلا جاز عليهما،

والله أعلم.

# بَابُ الخُلْع

# Chapter: A Release for Payment from the Wife

**554.** This is when the wife seeks to separate from her husband in return for remuneration from her or a third party.

**555.** The basis for this practice is based on the verse:

*"...but if you fear that they will not keep [within] the limits of Allāh, then there will be no blame on either of them if the woman opts to give something for her release..." (2:229)*

**556.** If a woman dislikes the mannerisms or the physical appearance of her husband and she fears she will not be able to fulfil his rights by staying with him, then there is no harm if she offers him remuneration in exchange for separation.

**557.** A release for payment is valid from any person whose divorce is valid with remuneration of any amount, small or large.

# بابُ الخُلْعِ

٥٥٤. وهُوَ فِراقُ زَوْجَتِهِ بِعِوَضٍ مِنها أوْ مِن غَيْرِها.

٥٥٥. والأصْلُ فِيهِ قَوْلُهُ تَعالى: ﴿فَإِنْ خِفْتُمْ أَلَّا يُقِيمَا
حُدُودَ ٱللَّهِ فَلَا جُنَاحَ عَلَيْهِمَا فِيمَا ٱفْتَدَتْ بِهِۦ﴾
[البَقَرَة: ٢٢٩]

٥٥٦. فَإذا كَرِهَتْ المرأةُ خُلُقَ زَوْجِها أو خَلْقه، وخافَتْ أَلّا
تُقِيمَ حُقُوقَهُ الواجِبَةَ بِإقامَتِها مَعَهُ، فلا بأسَ أن تبذِلَ له
عِوَضًا لِيُفارِقَها.

٥٥٧. ويَصِحُّ في كُلِّ قَلِيلٍ وكَثِيرٍ مِمَّنْ يَصِحُّ طَلاقُهُ.

**558.** However, if there is no fear that she cannot fulfil his rights, then the following *ḥadīth* states, "If a woman asks for a divorce without a valid reason, the fragrance of paradise will be forbidden for her." (Abū Dāwūd)

٥٥٨. فَإِنْ كَانَ لِغَيْرِ خَوْفٍ أَلَّا تُقِيمَ حُدُودَ اللهِ فَقَدْ وَرَدَ فِي الحَدِيثِ: «مَن سَأَلَتْ زَوجَها الطَّلاقَ مِن غَيرِ ما بَأْسٍ فَحَرامٌ عَلَيها رائِحَةُ الجَنَّةِ»

# كِتَابُ الطَّلَاق

# The Book of Divorce

**559.** Divorce is based upon the verse:

*"O Prophet, when any of you intend to divorce women, do so at a time when their prescribed waiting period can properly start, and calculate the period carefully..."* (65:1) alongside other texts from the Qurʾān and Sunnah.

**560.** Divorcing them when their *"prescribed waiting period can properly start"* has been explained in the ḥadīth of Ibn ʿUmar ﷺ whereby he divorced his wife while she was menstruating. ʿUmar ﷺ then asked the Prophet ﷺ about it, to which he ﷺ said, "Order him (your son) to take her back and keep her till she becomes pure and then to wait until she gets her next period and becomes pure again; if he wishes to keep her, he can do so, and if he wishes to divorce, her he can do so before having sexual intercourse with her. That is the prescribed period that Allāh ﷺ has fixed for the divorce of women." (Agreed upon) In another narration it states: "Order him to take her back then divorce her when she is either pure or pregnant." (Muslim) This proves that it is not permissible to divorce a woman while she is menstruating or when she is pure and he had intercourse with her, unless it is evident that she is pregnant.

# كِتابُ الطَّلاقِ

٥٥٩. والأصْلُ فِيهِ قَوْلُهُ تَعالى: ﴿يَأَيُّهَا ٱلنَّبِيُّ إِذَا طَلَّقْتُمُ ٱلنِّسَآءَ فَطَلِّقُوهُنَّ لِعِدَّتِهِنَّ وَأَحْصُوا۟ ٱلْعِدَّةَ﴾ [الطلاق: ١]

٥٦٠. وطَلاقُهُنَّ لِعِدَّتِهِنَّ، فَسَّرَهُ حَدِيثُ ابْنِ عُمَرَ، حَيْثُ طَلَّقَ زَوْجَتَهُ وهِيَ حائِضٌ، فَسَأَلَ عُمَرُ رضي الله عنه رسولَ اللهِ ﷺ عَنْ ذَلِكَ، فَقالَ: «مُرْهُ فَلْيُراجِعها ثُمَّ لِيَتْرُكها حَتّى تَطْهُرَ، ثُمَّ تَحِيضَ، ثُمَّ تَطْهُرَ، ثُمَّ إنْ شاءَ أمْسَكَ بَعْد، وإنْ شاءَ طَلَّقَ قَبْلَ أنْ يَمَسَّ، فَتِلْكَ العِدَّةُ الَّتِي أمَرَ اللهُ أنْ تُطَلَّقَ لَها النِّساءُ» مُتَّفَقٌ عَلَيْهِ، وفِي رِوايَةٍ: «مُرْهُ فَلْيُراجِعها ثُمَّ لِيُطَلِّقْها طاهِرًا أوْ حامِلًا».

وهَذا دَلِيلٌ عَلى أنَّهُ لا يَحِلُّ لَهُ أنْ يُطَلِّقَها وهِيَ حائِضٌ، أوْ فِي طُهْرٍ وطِئَ فِيهِ، إلّا إنْ تَبَيَّنَ حَمْلُها.

**561.** Divorce takes effect with every word that indicates divorce. These words can be:

1. *Ṣarīḥ* (explicit): These are words that give no meaning other than divorce, such as '*ṭalāq*' (divorce) and all the derivatives of the word. All words that have a similar meaning also apply here.
2. *Kināyah* (allusive): If he intended by the word to divorce her or there was some kind of indication to suggest that.

**562.** Divorce can either occur:

1. Immediately
2. Subject to a condition, such as saying, "When such and such time comes, you are divorced." Thus, when the stipulated event or circumstance occurs, the divorce becomes effective.

٥٦١. ويَقَعُ الطَّلاقُ بِكُلِّ لَفْظٍ دَلَّ عليه من:

١. صَريحٍ، لا يُفْهَمُ مِنهُ سِوى الطَّلاقِ، كَلَفْظِ: الطَّلاقِ، وما تَصَرَّفَ مِنهُ، وما كانَ مِثْلَهُ.

٢. وكِنايَةٍ، إذا نَوى بِها الطَّلاقَ، أو دَلَّتْ القَرينَةُ عَلى ذَلِكَ.

٥٦٢. ويَقَعُ الطَّلاقُ:

١. مُنْجَزًا.

٢. أو مُعَلَّقًا عَلى شَرْطٍ، كَقَوْلِهِ: إذا جاءَ الوَقْتُ الفُلانِيُّ فَأَنْتِ طالِقٌ، فَمَتى وُجِدَ الشَّرْطُ الذي عَلَّقَ عَلَيْهِ الطَّلاقَ وقع.

159

# The Revocable & Irrevocable Divorce

**563.** A free man possesses three pronouncements of divorce.

**564.** If he pronounces all three divorces, she will not be permissible for him until she legally marries another man and consummates the marriage with him. This is as per the statement of Allāh ﷻ:

*"Divorce may happen twice, and [each time] the wives are either to be kept in an acceptable manner or released in a wholesome way. It is not lawful for you to take back anything that you have given [your wives], except where both [of you] fear that they cannot maintain [the marriage] within the bounds set by God: if you [arbiters] suspect that the couple may not be able to do this, then there will be no blame on either of them if the woman opts to give something for her release. These are the bounds set by God: do not overstep them. Whoever oversteps God's bounds is from the wrongdoers.*

*If a husband re-divorces his wife after the second divorce, she will not be lawful for him until she has taken another husband; if that [husband] divorces her, there will be no blame if she and the first husband return to one another, provided they feel that they can*

*keep within the bounds set by God. These are God's bounds, which*
*He makes clear for those who know." (2:229:230)*

# فصل الطَّلاقِ البائِنِ والرَّجْعِي

٥٦٣. ويملك الحر ثلاث طلقات

٥٦٤. فإذا تمت له لم تحل له حتى تَنْكِحَ زَوْجًا غيره بِنِكَاحٍ صَحِيحٍ وَيَطأَها؛ لقوله تعالى: ﴿ٱلطَّلَٰقُ مَرَّتَانِۖ فَإِمْسَاكُۢ بِمَعْرُوفٍ أَوْ تَسْرِيحُۢ بِإِحْسَٰنٍۗ وَلَا يَحِلُّ لَكُمْ أَن تَأْخُذُواْ مِمَّآ ءَاتَيْتُمُوهُنَّ شَيْـًٔا إِلَّآ أَن يَخَافَآ أَلَّا يُقِيمَا حُدُودَ ٱللَّهِۖ فَإِنْ خِفْتُمْ أَلَّا يُقِيمَا حُدُودَ ٱللَّهِ فَلَا جُنَاحَ عَلَيْهِمَا فِيمَا ٱفْتَدَتْ بِهِۦۗ تِلْكَ حُدُودُ ٱللَّهِ فَلَا تَعْتَدُوهَاۚ وَمَن يَتَعَدَّ حُدُودَ ٱللَّهِ فَأُوْلَٰٓئِكَ هُمُ ٱلظَّٰلِمُونَ ۝ فَإِن طَلَّقَهَا فَلَا تَحِلُّ لَهُۥ مِنۢ بَعْدُ حَتَّىٰ تَنكِحَ زَوْجًا غَيْرَهُۥۗ فَإِن طَلَّقَهَا فَلَا جُنَاحَ عَلَيْهِمَآ أَن يَتَرَاجَعَآ إِن ظَنَّآ أَن يُقِيمَا حُدُودَ ٱللَّهِۗ وَتِلْكَ حُدُودُ ٱللَّهِ يُبَيِّنُهَا لِقَوْمٍ يَعْلَمُونَ ۝﴾ [البَقَرة]

**565.** The *bāʾin* (irrevocable divorce) occurs in four ways:

1. The above-mentioned case.
2. If he divorced her before consummation of the marriage. This is as per the saying of Allāh ﷻ

*"O believers, you have no right to expect a waiting period when you marry believing women and then divorce them before you have touched them: make provision for them and release them in an honourable way."* (33:49)

3. If the marriage was invalid.
4. If the separation was in exchange for remuneration.

**566.** Everything other than the aforementioned will be considered *rajʿī* (a revocable divorce). The husband can thus take her back as long as she is in her *ʿiddah*. This is based upon the verse:

*"And their husbands have more right to take them back during this [period] if they want reconciliation."* (2:228)

**567.** A woman who has been divorced in the revocable form has the same rulings of a normal wife applied to her except in the case of equal division of the husband's time.

٥٦٥. ويقع الطلاق بائنًا في أربع مسائل:

١. هذه إحداها.

٢. وإذا طلق قبل الدخول؛ لقوله تعالى: ﴿يَٰٓأَيُّهَا ٱلَّذِينَ ءَامَنُوٓاْ إِذَا نَكَحْتُمُ ٱلْمُؤْمِنَٰتِ ثُمَّ طَلَّقْتُمُوهُنَّ مِن قَبْلِ أَن تَمَسُّوهُنَّ فَمَا لَكُمْ عَلَيْهِنَّ مِنْ عِدَّةٍ تَعْتَدُّونَهَا﴾ [الأحزاب: ٤٩]

٣. وإذا كان في نكاح فاسد.

٤. وإذا كانَ عَلى عِوَضٍ.

٥٦٦. وما سِوى ذَلِكَ، فهو رجعي، يملك الزوج رجعة زَوْجَتِهِ ما دامَتْ في العِدَّةِ؛ لِقَوْلِهِ تعالى: ﴿وَبُعُولَتُهُنَّ أَحَقُّ بِرَدِّهِنَّ فِي ذَٰلِكَ إِنْ أَرَادُوٓاْ إِصْلَٰحًا﴾ [البقرة: ٢٢٨]

٥٦٧. والرجعية حكمها حكم الزوجات، إلا في وجوب القسم.

**568.** It is legislated to announce the marriage, the divorce, the *rajʿah* (taking back of a wife), and having witnesses for it. This is as per the verse:

*"Call two just witnesses from your people."* (65:2)

**569.** The Prophet ﷺ said, "There are three things that, whether undertaken seriously or in jest, are treated seriously: marriage, divorce, and taking back a wife [after a revocable divorce]. (Abū Dāwūd and others)

**570.** In a *marfūʿ ḥadīth*, Ibn ʿAbbās ﷺ narrated, "Indeed Allāh ﷻ has overlooked the actions of my *ummah* that were committed as mistakes or due to forgetfulness or coercion." (Ibn Mājah)

٥٦٨. والمشْرُوعُ إعْلانُ النِّكاحِ والطَّلاقِ والرَّجْعَةِ، والإشْهادُ عَلى ذَلِكَ؛

لِقَوْلِهِ تَعالى: ﴿وَأَشْهِدُواْ ذَوَىْ عَدْلٍ مِّنكُمْ﴾ [الطَّلاق:٢]

٥٦٩. وفِي الحَدِيثِ: «ثَلاثٌ جِدُّهُنَّ جِدٌّ وهَزْلُهُنَّ جِدٌّ: النِّكاحُ، والطَّلاقُ، والرَّجْعَةُ» رَواهُ الأَرْبَعَةُ إلّا النَّسائِيُّ.

٥٧٠. وفِي حَدِيثِ ابْنِ عَبّاسٍ، مَرْفُوعًا: «إنَّ اللهَ وضَعَ عَنْ أُمَّتي الخَطَأَ والنِّسْيانَ وما اسْتُكْرِهُوا عَلَيهِ» رواه ابن ماجه.

# بَابُ الإِيلَاء والظِّهَار واللِّعَان

# Chapter: Vow of Continence, Injurious Assimilation & Imprecation

## (Vow of Continence: *Īlā*)

**571.** *Īlā* is to vow not have intercourse with one's wife for an indefinite period of time, or for a period of time lasting more than four months.

**572.** The husband must have sexual intercourse with his wife if she requests it. He will be given four months to respond to the request.

- If he has sexual intercourse with her, he has to expiate for breaking an oath.
- If he still refuses to have intercourse with her after that (i.e. four months), he will be made to divorce her, as per the saying of Allāh ﷻ:

*"For those who swear that they will not approach their wives, there shall be a waiting period of four months: if they go back, remember God will be most forgiving and merciful, but if they are determined to divorce, remember that God hears and knows all." (2:226-7)*

# بابُ الإيلاءِ والظّهارِ واللّعانِ

## الإيلاءُ

**٥٧١**. فالإيلاءُ: أَنْ يَحْلِفَ عَلى تَرْكِ وطْءِ زَوْجَتِهِ أَبَدًا، أَوْ مُدَّةً تَزِيدُ عَلى أَرْبَعَةِ أَشْهُرٍ.

**٥٧٢**. فَإذا طَلَبَتْ الزَّوْجَةُ حَقَّها مِن الوَطْءِ، أُمِرَ بِوَطْئِها، وضُرِبَتْ لَهُ أَرْبَعَةُ أَشْهُرٍ:

– فَإِنْ وطِئَ كَفَّرَ كَفَّارَةَ يَمِينٍ،

– وإِنْ امْتَنَعَ أُلْزِمَ بِالطَّلاقِ؛

لِقَوْلِهِ تَعالى: ﴿لِّلَّذِينَ يُؤْلُونَ مِن نِّسَآئِهِمْ تَرَبُّصُ أَرْبَعَةِ أَشْهُرٍ فَإِن فَآءُو فَإِنَّ ٱللَّهَ غَفُورٌ رَّحِيمٌ ۝ وَإِنْ عَزَمُواْ ٱلطَّلَقَ فَإِنَّ ٱللَّهَ سَمِيعٌ عَلِيمٌ ۝﴾ [الْبَقَرَة]

167

## (Injurious Assimilation: *Ẓihār*)

**573.** *Ẓihār* is to say to one's wife, "You are to me like the backside of my mother" and other similar phrases that make one's wife forbidden.

**574.** Such statements are considered *munkar* (evil) and *zūr* (false).

**575.** The wife does not become prohibited to him by it. However, he is not allowed to touch her until he does what Allāh ﷻ commands:

*"Those of you who say such a thing to their wives, then go back on what they have said, must free a slave before the couple may touch one another again - this is what you are commanded to do, and God is fully aware of what you do - but anyone who does not have the means should fast continuously for two months before they touch each other, and anyone unable to do this should feed sixty needy people. This is so that you may have [true] faith in God and His Messenger. These are the bounds set by God: grievous torment awaits those who ignore them."* (58:3-4)

# الظِّهار

**٥٧٣.** والظِّهارُ أنْ يَقُولَ لِزَوْجَتِهِ: أنْتِ عَلَيَّ كَظَهْرِ أمي، ونحوه من ألفاظ التحريم الصريحة لزوجته.

**٥٧٤.** فهو منكر وزور.

**٥٧٥.** ولا تَحْرُمُ الزوجة بذلك، لكن لا يحل له أن يمسها حتى يفعل ما أمره الله به في قوله: ﴿وَٱلَّذِينَ يُظَٰهِرُونَ مِن نِّسَآئِهِمْ ثُمَّ يَعُودُونَ لِمَا قَالُوا فَتَحْرِيرُ رَقَبَةٍ مِّن قَبْلِ أَن يَتَمَآسَّا ذَٰلِكُمْ تُوعَظُونَ بِهِۦۚ وَٱللَّهُ بِمَا تَعْمَلُونَ خَبِيرٌ ۝ فَمَن لَّمْ يَجِدْ فَصِيَامُ شَهْرَيْنِ مُتَتَابِعَيْنِ مِن قَبْلِ أَن يَتَمَآسَّاۖ فَمَن لَّمْ يَسْتَطِعْ فَإِطْعَامُ سِتِّينَ مِسْكِينًاۚ ذَٰلِكَ لِتُؤْمِنُوا بِٱللَّهِ وَرَسُولِهِۦۚ وَتِلْكَ حُدُودُ ٱللَّهِۗ وَلِلْكَٰفِرِينَ عَذَابٌ أَلِيمٌ ۝﴾ [المجادلة]

Thus, he must:

1. Free a Muslim slave that is free from any defect that can affect his work.
2. If he cannot find a slave, he must fast two consecutive months.
3. If he cannot manage that, he must feed sixty poor people.

**576.** This applies whether the *ẓihār* was unrestricted or limited to a certain time period, such as *Ramaḍān*.

**577.** Expiation is due if a person makes a slave, food, or clothing and so on, unlawful to oneself, as per the saying of Allāh ﷻ:

*"O You who believe, do not forbid the good things God has made lawful to you - do not exceed the limits: God does not love those who exceed the limits - but eat the lawful and good things that God provides for you. Be mindful of God, in whom you believe.*
*God does not take you [to task] for what is thoughtless in your oaths [rather] only for your binding oaths: the atonement for breaking an oath is to feed ten poor people with food equivalent to what you would normally give your own families, or to clothe them, or to set free a slave - if a person cannot find the means, he should fast for three days. This is the atonement for breaking your oaths - keep your oaths. In this way God makes clear His revelations to you so that you may be thankful."* (5:87-89)

١. فيعتق رقبة مؤمنة سالمة من العيوب الضارة بالعمل.

٢. فإن لم يجد، صام شهرين متتابعين.

٣. فإن لم يستطع، أطعم ستين مسكينًا.

٥٧٦. وسواءٌ كان الظهار مطلقًا، أو مؤقتًا بوقت كرمضان ونحوه.

٥٧٧. وأمّا تَحْرِيمُ المِمْلُوكَةِ والطَّعامِ واللِّباسِ وغَيْرِها فَفِيهِ كَفَّارَةُ يَمِينٍ؛ لِقَوْلِهِ تَعالى: ﴿يَٰٓأَيُّهَا ٱلَّذِينَ ءَامَنُواْ لَا تُحَرِّمُواْ طَيِّبَٰتِ مَآ أَحَلَّ ٱللَّهُ لَكُمْ وَلَا تَعْتَدُوٓاْ إِنَّ ٱللَّهَ لَا يُحِبُّ ٱلْمُعْتَدِينَ ۝ وَكُلُواْ مِمَّا رَزَقَكُمُ ٱللَّهُ حَلَٰلًا طَيِّبًا وَٱتَّقُواْ ٱللَّهَ ٱلَّذِىٓ أَنتُم بِهِۦ مُؤْمِنُونَ ۝ لَا يُؤَاخِذُكُمُ ٱللَّهُ بِٱللَّغْوِ فِىٓ أَيْمَٰنِكُمْ وَلَٰكِن يُؤَاخِذُكُم بِمَا عَقَّدتُّمُ ٱلْأَيْمَٰنَّ فَكَفَّٰرَتُهُۥٓ إِطْعَامُ عَشَرَةِ مَسَٰكِينَ مِنْ أَوْسَطِ مَا تُطْعِمُونَ أَهْلِيكُمْ أَوْ كِسْوَتُهُمْ أَوْ تَحْرِيرُ رَقَبَةٍ فَمَن لَّمْ يَجِدْ فَصِيَامُ ثَلَٰثَةِ أَيَّامٍ ذَٰلِكَ كَفَّٰرَةُ أَيْمَٰنِكُمْ إِذَا حَلَفْتُمْ وَٱحْفَظُوٓاْ أَيْمَٰنَكُمْ كَذَٰلِكَ يُبَيِّنُ ٱللَّهُ لَكُمْ ءَايَٰتِهِۦ لَعَلَّكُمْ تَشْكُرُونَ ۝﴾ [المائدة]

(Imprecation: *liʿān*)

**578.** If a man accuses his wife of committing adultery, he will be punished by eighty lashes unless:

1. He can produce evidence; namely, four just witnesses, in which case she will be punished, or
2. He swears an oath, in which case he is no longer liable to be punished.

**579.** The description of the imprecation is in accordance with what Allāh ﷻ mentioned in *Sūrah al-Nūr:*

*"As for those who accuse their own wives of adultery but have no other witnesses, let each one call God to witness that he is telling the truth four times, and on the fifth, call God to curse him if he is lying. Punishment shall be averted from his wife if she in turn calls God to witness that her husband is lying four times and, on the fifth, calls God to curse her if he is telling the truth."* (24:6-9)

1. He therefore has to bear witness five times, swearing by Allāh ﷻ that she is an adulteress. And he should say in the fifth instance, "May the curse of Allāh ﷻ be upon him if he is from the liars."

# اللِّعانُ

**٥٧٨.** وأمّا اللِّعانُ فإذا رَمى الرَّجُلُ زَوجَتَهُ بالزنى فَعَلَيهِ حَدُّ القَذْفِ ثَمانُونَ جَلْدَةً إلّا:

١. أَنْ يُقِيمَ البَيِّنَةَ: أَرْبَعَةَ شُهُودٍ عُدُولٍ، فَيُقامُ عَلَيها الحَدُّ.

٢. أَوْ يُلاعِنُ فَيَسْقُطُ عَنْهُ حَدُّ القَذْفِ.

**٥٧٩.** وصِفَةُ اللِّعانِ عَلى ما ذَكَرَ اللهُ في سُورَةِ النُّورِ:

﴿وَٱلَّذِينَ يَرْمُونَ أَزْوَٰجَهُمْ وَلَمْ يَكُن لَّهُمْ شُهَدَآءُ إِلَّآ أَنفُسُهُمْ فَشَهَٰدَةُ أَحَدِهِمْ أَرْبَعُ شَهَٰدَٰتٍ بِٱللَّهِ إِنَّهُۥ لَمِنَ ٱلصَّٰدِقِينَ ۝ وَٱلْخَٰمِسَةُ أَنَّ لَعْنَتَ ٱللَّهِ عَلَيْهِ إِن كَانَ مِنَ ٱلْكَٰذِبِينَ ۝ وَيَدْرَؤُاْ عَنْهَا ٱلْعَذَابَ أَن تَشْهَدَ أَرْبَعَ شَهَٰدَٰتٍ بِٱللَّهِ إِنَّهُۥ لَمِنَ ٱلْكَٰذِبِينَ ۝ وَٱلْخَٰمِسَةَ أَنَّ غَضَبَ ٱللَّهِ عَلَيْهَآ إِن كَانَ مِنَ ٱلصَّٰدِقِينَ ۝﴾

[سورة النور]

١. فَيَشْهَدُ خَمْسَ شَهاداتٍ بِاللهِ إنَّها لَزانِيَةٌ، ويَقُولُ في الخامِسَةِ: وإنَّ لَعْنَةَ اللهِ عَلَيْهِ إنْ كانَ مِنَ الكاذِبينَ.

2. Thereafter, she is to swear by Allāh ﷻ five times that he is from the liars. And she should say in the fifth instance, "May the wrath of Allāh ﷻ be upon her if he is from the truthful."

**580.** Once the imprecation is complete:

1. The legal punishment (*ḥadd*) will be dropped from the husband.
2. She will not be punished for adultery.
3. Both will then be separated and will never be allowed to re-marry.
4. The child will not be attributed to him if the child was mentioned in the imprecation.

And Allāh ﷻ knows best.

٢. ثُمَّ تَشْهَدُ هِيَ خَمْسَ مَرَّاتٍ بِاللهِ إِنَّهُ لِمَن الكاذِبِينَ، وتَقُولُ فِي الخامِسَةِ: وإنَّ غَضِبَ اللهِ عَلَيْها إنْ كانَ مِن الصَّادِقِينَ.

٥٨٠. فَإذا تَمَّ اللِّعانُ:

١. سَقَطَ عَنْهُ الحد،

٢. واندرأ عنها العذاب،

٣. وحصلت الفرقة بينهما والتحريم المؤبد.

٤. وانْتَفى الوَلَدُ إذا ذُكِرَ فِي اللِّعان.

واللهُ أعلم.

كِتَابُ العِدَد والاِسْتِبْرَاء

# The Book of ʿIdad (post-marital waiting period) & Istibrāʾ (verification of non-pregnancy)

**581.** The ʿiddah is the waiting period a woman must observe after separating from her husband due to his death or divorce.

**582.** A woman must observe the ʿiddah due to her husband's death in all cases:

- If she was pregnant, her ʿiddah lasts until she gives birth as per the saying of Allāh ﷻ:

*"...the waiting period of those who are pregnant will be until they deliver their burden..."* (65:4)

This is a general ruling regarding separation due to death or divorce.

- If not pregnant, her ʿiddah lasts for four months and ten days.

# كِتابُ العِدَدِ والاسْتِبْراءِ

٥٨١. العِدَّةُ تَرَبُّصُ مَن فارَقَها زَوْجُها بِموتٍ أوْ طَلاقٍ.

٥٨٢. فالمفارَقَةُ بالموْتِ إذا ماتَ عَنْها تَعْتَدُّ عَلى كُلِّ حالٍ:

- فَإنْ كانَتْ حامِلًا فَعِدَّتُها وضْعُها جَميعَ ما في بَطْنِها؛ لِقَوْلِهِ تَعالى: ﴿وَأُوْلَٰتُ ٱلْأَحْمَالِ أَجَلُهُنَّ أَن يَضَعْنَ حَمْلَهُنَّ﴾ [الطَّلاق: ٤]

وهَذا عامٌّ في المفارَقَةِ بِمَوْتٍ أوْ حَياةٍ.

- وإنْ لَمْ تَكُنْ حامِلًا فَعِدَّتُها أرْبَعَةَ أشْهرٍ وعَشَرَةُ أيّامٍ.

**583.** During this period she mourns by:

1. Avoiding beautification, perfume, wearing jewellery and adorning oneself with henna, and so on.
2. Staying at the home she was living in with her husband before he passed away. She should not leave the home except due to a pressing need during the day. This is due to the saying of Allāh ﷻ:

*"If any of you die and leave widows, the widows should wait for four months and ten nights before remarrying."* (2:234)

**584.** In the case of separation whilst both are alive:

1. If he divorced her before consummating the marriage, then she does not observe the ʿiddah as per the saying of Allāh ﷻ:

*"O you who have believed, you have no right to expect a waiting period when you marry believing women and then divorce them before you have touched them: make provision for them and release them in an honourable way."* (33:49)

٥٨٣. ويَلْزَمُ في مُدَّةِ هَذِهِ العِدَّةِ أَنْ تُحِدَّ المرْأَةُ:

١. بِأَنْ تَتْرُكَ الزِّينَةَ والطِّيبِ والحُلِيَّ، والتحسين بحناء ونحوه

٢. وأن تلزم بيتها الذي مات زوجها وهي فيه، فلا تخرج منه إلا لحاجتها نَهارًا؛ لقوله تعالى: ﴿وَٱلَّذِينَ يُتَوَفَّوْنَ مِنكُمْ وَيَذَرُونَ أَزْوَٰجًا يَتَرَبَّصْنَ بِأَنفُسِهِنَّ أَرْبَعَةَ أَشْهُرٍ وَعَشْرًا﴾ [البقرة: ٢٣٤]

٥٨٤. وأما المفارقة في حال الحياة:

١. فإذا طلقها قبل أن يدخل بها، فلا عدة له عليها؛ لقوله تعالى: ﴿يَٰٓأَيُّهَا ٱلَّذِينَ ءَامَنُوٓا۟ إِذَا نَكَحْتُمُ ٱلْمُؤْمِنَٰتِ ثُمَّ طَلَّقْتُمُوهُنَّ مِن قَبْلِ أَن تَمَسُّوهُنَّ فَمَا لَكُمْ عَلَيْهِنَّ مِنْ عِدَّةٍ تَعْتَدُّونَهَا﴾ [الأحزاب: ٤٩]

2.  If he divorces her after consummating the marriage or by being alone with her, the following will apply:

A.  If she is pregnant, her *ʿiddah* is until she gives birth, whether the duration is long or short.

B.  If she is not pregnant:

   o  If she menstruates, her *ʿiddah* is for three complete menstrual periods, as per the saying of Allāh ﷻ:

*"Divorced women must wait for three monthly periods before remarrying."* (2:228)

   o  The *ʿiddah* for a woman who does not menstruate, whether prepubescent, post-menopausal, or a woman who generally does not menstruate, is three months as per the saying of Allāh ﷻ:

*"If you are in doubt, the period of waiting will be three months for those women who have ceased menstruating and for those who have not [yet] menstruated; the waiting period of those who are pregnant will be until they deliver their burden: God makes things easy for those who are mindful of Him."* (65:4)

٢. وإن كان قد دخل بها أو خلا بها:

أ. فإن كانت حاملًا فعدتها وضع حملها، قصرت المدة أو طالت.

ب. وإن لم تكن حاملًا:

فإن كانت تحيض فعدتها ثلاث حِيَضٍ كاملة؛ لقوله تعالى: ﴿وَٱلۡمُطَلَّقَٰتُ يَتَرَبَّصۡنَ بِأَنفُسِهِنَّ ثَلَٰثَةَ قُرُوٓءٖ﴾ [البقرة: ٢٢٨] وإن لم تكن تحيض كالصغيرة، ومن لم تحض، والآيسة فعدتها ثلاثة أشهر؛

لقوله تعالى: ﴿وَٱلَّٰٓـِٔي يَئِسۡنَ مِنَ ٱلۡمَحِيضِ مِن نِّسَآئِكُمۡ إِنِ ٱرۡتَبۡتُمۡ فَعِدَّتُهُنَّ ثَلَٰثَةُ أَشۡهُرٖ وَٱلَّٰٓـِٔي لَمۡ يَحِضۡنَۚ﴾ [الطلاق: ٤]

- If she normally menstruates but her periods stopped for a reason such as breastfeeding, then she should wait until her periods return and then observe the ʿiddah.
- If her periods stop and she does not know the cause behind it, she should wait nine months in case she is not pregnant. After that she should observe the ʿiddah for three months.
- If she begins to suspect pregnancy after the ʿiddah finished due to signs of pregnancy, she should not marry until she no longer suspects it.

585. The wife of a husband who is missing should wait until the verdict of his death is given according to the judgment of a judge; thereafter, she should observe the ʿiddah.

586. It is not obligatory to financially support her unless:

1. She has been divorced in a revocable fashion.
2. There was separation whilst he was alive, and she is pregnant. This is as per the saying of Allāh ﷻ:

*"If they are pregnant, maintain them until they deliver their burdens."* (65:6)

- فَإِنْ كَانَتْ تَحِيضُ وَارْتَفَعَ حَيْضُهَا لِرَضَاعٍ وَنَحْوِهِ، انتظرت حتى يعود الحيض فتعتد به.

- وَإِنْ ارْتَفَعَ وَلَا تَدْرِي مَا رَفَعَهُ، انْتَظَرَتْ تِسْعَةَ أَشْهُرٍ احْتِيَاطًا لِلْحَمْلِ، ثُمَّ اعْتَدَّتْ بِثَلَاثَةِ أَشْهُرٍ.

- وَإِذَا ارْتَابَتْ بَعْدَ انْقِضَاءِ العِدَّةِ لِظُهُورِ أماراتِ الحَمْلِ لَمْ تَتَزَوَّجْ حَتَّى تَزُولَ الرِّيبَةُ.

٥٨٥. وامْرَأَةُ المَفْقُودِ تَنْتَظِرُ حَتَّى يُحْكَمَ بِمَوْتِهِ، بِحَسَبِ اجْتِهادِ الحاكِمِ ثُمَّ تَعْتَدُّ.

٥٨٦. ولا تَجِبُ النَّفَقَةُ إِلَّا:

١. لِلْمُعْتَدَّةِ الرَّجعِيَّةِ،

٢. أَوْ لِمَن فارَقَها زَوْجُها فِي الحَياةِ وهِيَ حامِلٌ؛ لِقَوْلِهِ تَعالى: ﴿وَإِن كُنَّ أُوْلَٰتِ حَمْلٍ فَأَنفِقُواْ عَلَيْهِنَّ حَتَّىٰ يَضَعْنَ حَمْلَهُنَّ﴾ [الطَّلَاقُ: ٦]

## Istibrāʾ

**587.** *Al Istibrāʾ* is the waiting period of a slave if her master had sexual relations with her.

**588.** No one should have sexual intercourse with her after him, whether husband or master until:

1. She completes one period
2. If she was from those who do not menstruate, she should wait for one month
3. If pregnant, until she gives birth

٥٨٧. وأمّا الاسْتِبْراءِ: فَهُوَ تربص الأمة التي كان سيدها يطؤها.

٥٨٨. فلا يطؤها بعده زوج أو سيد:

١. حتى تحيض حيضة واحدة،

٢. وإن لم تكن من ذوات الحيض تستبرأ بشهر،

٣. أو وضع حملها إن كانت حاملًا،

# بَابُ النَّفَقَاتِ لِلزَّوْجَاتِ والأَقَارِبِ والمَمَالِيك والحَضَانَة

# Chapter: Financial Support for Wives, Relatives, Slaves & Custody

**589.** It is upon the husband to financially support his wife, clothe her, and give her a dwelling place, all in accordance to what is customary and in accordance with his financial situation.

This is per the saying of Allāh ﷻ:

*"Let the wealthy man spend according to his wealth. But let him whose provision is restricted spend according to what God has given him: God does not burden any soul with more than He has given it - after hardship, God will bring ease."* (65:7)

**590.** The husband is required to provide the necessary financial support to his wife if she requests it.

Jābir ﷺ related in a *ḥadīth* reported in Muslim, "They have a right upon you to be provided for and clothed in a fair manner."

# بابُ النَّفقاتِ للزَّوجاتِ والأقاربِ والمَماليكِ والحَضانةِ

٥٨٩. عَلى الإنْسانِ نَفَقَةُ زَوْجَتِهِ وكِسْوَتُها ومَسْكَنُها بالمَعْروفِ بِحَسَبِ حالِ الزَّوجِ؛ لِقَوْلِهِ تَعالى: ﴿لِيُنفِقْ ذُو سَعَةٍ مِّن سَعَتِهِۦۖ وَمَن قُدِرَ عَلَيْهِ رِزْقُهُۥ فَلْيُنفِقْ مِمَّآ ءَاتَىٰهُ ٱللَّهُ لَا يُكَلِّفُ ٱللَّهُ نَفْسًا إِلَّا مَآ ءَاتَىٰهَاۚ﴾ [الطَّلاقُ: ٧]

٥٩٠. ويَلْزِمُ بالواجِبِ مِن ذَلِكَ إذا طَلَبَتْ، وفِي حَدِيثِ جابِرٍ الَّذِي رَواهُ مُسْلِمٌ: «ولَهُنَّ عَلَيْكُمْ رِزْقُهُنَّ وكِسْوَتُهُنَّ بالمَعْرُوفِ»

187

**591.** It is obligatory upon one to:

1. Financially support one's poor parents and their ascendants as well as one's descendants if one has the financial means to do so.
2. Financially support those who inherit from him by either a prescribed share or by being a residual heir.

**592.** The Prophet ﷺ said, "A slave has a right to be fed and clothed, and he should not be burdened with work more than he can bear." (Muslim)

**593.** If a slave requests to get married, it is obligatory upon the master to marry him off.

**594.** It is obligatory to feed and provide water to one's animals. They should not be burdened with something that will harm them.

The Prophet ﷺ said, "It is enough of a sin to withhold sustenance from those under one's care." (Muslim)

٥٩١. وعلى الإنسان:

١. نفقة أصوله وفروعه الفقراء إذا كان غنيًّا،

٢. وكَذَلِكَ مَن يَرِثُهُ بِفَرْضٍ أوْ تَعْصِيب.

٥٩٢. وفِي الحَدِيثِ: «لِلْمَمْلُوكِ طَعامُهُ وكِسْوَتُهُ، ولا يُكَلَّفُ مِن العَمَلِ إلَّا ما يُطِيقُ» رَواهُ مُسْلِم.

٥٩٣. وإنْ طَلَبَ التَّزَوُّجَ زَوَّجَهُ وُجُوبًا.

٥٩٤. وعَلَى الإنْسانِ أنْ يُقِيتَ بَهائِمه طَعامًا وشَرابًا، ولا يُكَلِّفُها ما يَضُرُّها.

وفِي الحَدِيثِ: «كَفى بِالمرءِ إثْمًا أنْ يَحْبِسَ عَمَّنْ يَمْلِكُ قُوتَهُ» رَواهُ مُسْلِم

## Custody

**595.** *Ḥaḍānah* is to see to the needs of one's children and protect children from that which will harm them.

**596.** It is obligatory upon the one who is obliged to support them financially.

**597.** However, the mother has more right to the child, whether a son or daughter, if they are less than seven years old.

**598.** Once the child has reached the age of seven:

1. If the child is a boy, he is to be given the choice of either parent he wishes to stay with.
2. If the child is a female, then it is dependent upon the one who can see to her needs best and look after her better, whether it is the mother or father.

**599.** The custody of children should not be given to someone who cannot protect and look after them.

٥٩٥. والحَضانَةُ: هِيَ حِفْظُ الطِّفْلِ عَمّا يَضُرُّهُ، والقِيامُ بِمَصالِحِهِ.

٥٩٦. وهِيَ واجِبَةٌ عَلى مَن تَجِبُ عَلَيْهِ النفقة.

٥٩٧. ولكن الأم أحق بولدها ذكرًا كان أو أنثى إن كان دون سبع.

٥٩٨. فإذا بلغ سبعًا:

١. فإن كان ذكرًا خير بين أبويه، فكان مع من اختار.

٢. وإن كانت أنثي فعند من يقوم بمصلحتها من أمها أو أبيها.

٥٩٩. ولا يُتْرَكُ المَحْضُونُ بِيَدِ مَن لا يَصُونُهُ ويصلحه

# كِتَابُ الأَطْعِمَة

# The Book of Foods

**600.** Food is of two types: meat and non-meat:

1.  As for non-meat food - such as grains and fruits - they are all permissible except that what is harmful, such as poison and the like.

All drinks are permissible except for that which intoxicates - which is prohibited to drink whether in small or large amounts - as per the ḥadīth, "Every intoxicant is prohibited; if a large amount of it causes intoxication, a small amount of it is prohibited."

If wine turns into vinegar, it becomes permissible to consume.

2.  Animals are of two types:

A. Sea animals. Everything in the sea is permissible, whether alive or dead.

Allāh ﷻ says, *"It is permitted for you to catch and eat seafood..."* (5:96)

# كِتاب الأطْعِمَةِ

٦٠٠. وهِيَ نَوْعانِ: حَيَوانٌ وغَيْرُهُ:

١. فَأمّا غَيْرُ الحَيَوانِ مِن الحُبُوبِ والثِّمارِ وغَيْرِها فَكُلُّهُ مُباحٌ، إلّا ما فِيهِ مَضَرَّةٌ، كالسُّمِّ ونَحْوِهِ، والأشْرِبَةُ كُلُّها مُباحَة إلّا ما أسْكَرَ، فإنه يحرم كثيره وقليله؛ لِحَدِيثٍ: «كُلُّ مُسْكِرٍ حَرامٌ، وما أسْكَرَ مِنهُ الفَرَقُ فَمِلْءُ الكَفِّ مِنهُ حَرامٌ» وإنْ انْقَلَبَتْ الخَمْرُ خَلًّا حَلَّتْ.

٢. والحَيَوانُ قِسْمانِ:

أ- بَحْرِيٌّ، فَيَحِلُّ كُلُّ ما في البَحْرِ حَيًّا ومَيِّتًا؛ قالَ تَعالى: ﴿أُحِلَّ لَكُمْ صَيْدُ ٱلْبَحْرِ وَطَعَامُهُ﴾ [المائدة: ٩٦]

B. Land animals. The original ruling of land animals is that they are permissible except that which Allāh ﷻ prohibited, such as:

- That which is mentioned in the *ḥadīth* of Ibn ʿAbbās ﷺ, "Predatory animals with canines are forbidden to eat."
- The Prophet ﷺ also forbade eating birds that have talons. (Muslim)
- He ﷺ also prohibited eating domestic donkeys. (Agreed upon)
- He ﷺ prohibited killing four creatures: ants, bees, hoopoes, and shrikes. (Aḥmad and Abū Dāwūd)
- All repulsive creatures such as insects are prohibited to consume.
- The Prophet ﷺ prohibited the eating of the *jallālah* (an animal that feeds on impurities) or drinking its milk, unless they are detained for three days and are fed pure food.

ب- وأمَّا البَرِّيُّ: فالأصلُ فِيهِ الحِلُّ، إلَّا ما نص عليه الشارع، فمنها:

- ما في الحديث اِبْنِ عَبَّاسٍ: «كُلِّ ذِي نابٍ مِن السِّباعِ فَأَكَلُهُ حَرامٌ»

- «ونَهى عَنْ كُلِّ ذِي مِخْلَبٍ مِن الطَّيْرِ» رَواهُ مُسْلِمُ.

- «ونَهى عَنْ لُحُومِ الحُمُرِ الأَهْلِيَّةِ». مُتَّفَقٌ عَلَيْهِ.

- «ونَهى عَنْ قَتْلِ أَرْبَعٍ مِن الدَّوابِّ: النَّمْلَةُ، والنحلة، والهدد والصُّرَدُ» رَواهُ أَحْمَدُ وأَبُو داوُدَ.

- وجَمِيعُ الخبائث محرمة كالحشرات ونحوها.

- ونَهى النَّبِيُّ ﷺ عن الجلالة وألبانها حتى تُحبس، وتطعم الطاهر ثلاثًا.

195

# بَابُ الذَّكَاة والصَّيْد

# Chapter: Slaughtering & Hunting

601. Permissible animals are not considered permissible to eat until they have been slaughtered, except for fish and locust.

602. The following matters are stipulated when slaughtering:

1. The slaughterer must be a Muslim or from the People of The Book (i.e. Jews and Christians).
2. The knife must be sharp (to as not to prolong the death).
3. The blood must gush forth from the body.
4. The trachea and the oesophagus must be cut.
5. The name of Allāh ﷻ must be mentioned when slaughtering.

603. The same is stipulated for hunting, except that it is allowed to incapacitate the hunted animal by targeting any part of its body.

604. If an animal is usually slaughtered but fled and thus was unable to be slaughtered, it can also be hunted.

# بابُ الذَّكاةُ والصَّيْدُ

**٦٠١.** الحَيواناتُ المباحةُ لا تُباحُ بِدُونِ الذَّكاةِ إلّا السَّمَكَ والجَرادَ.

**٦٠٢.** ويُشْتَرَطُ في الذَّكاةِ:

١. أنْ يَكونَ المذَكِّيَ مُسْلِمًا أوْ كِتابِيًّا.

٢. وأن يكون بمحدد.

٣. وأنْ يُنْهِرَ الدَّمَ.

٤. وأنْ يَقْطَعَ الحُلْقُومَ والمريءَ.

٥. وأنْ يَذْكُرَ اِسْمَ اللهِ عَلَيْهِ.

**٦٠٣.** وكَذَلِكَ يُشْتَرَطُ في الصَّيْدِ، إلّا أنَّهُ يَحِلُّ بِعَقْرِهِ في أي موضع من بدنه.

**٦٠٤.** ومِثلُ الصَّيْدِ ما نَفَرَ وعَجَزَ عَنْ ذَبْحِهِ.

**605.** Rāfiʾ ibn Khadīj ﷺ reported in a *marfūʿ ḥadīth*, "If the killing tool causes blood to gush out and if Allāh's ﷻ name is mentioned, eat [the sacrificed animal]. However, do not slaughter with a tooth or a nail. As for the tooth, then it is a bone, and as for the nail, then it is the knife of the Ethiopians." (Agreed upon)

**606.** It is permissible to used trained hunting dogs to hunt with on condition that its owner has sufficient control over it i.e. if its owner sends it to hunt, it goes, and if he restrains it, it holds back, and if it grabs the prey, it does not eat it. The owner of the dog should pronounce the name of Allāh ﷻ when he sends it.

**607.** ʿAdiyy Ibn Ḥatim ﷺ narrated that the Prophet ﷺ said, "When you send your trained dog, mention the name of Allāh ﷻ upon it.

- If it catches the prey and you find it alive, slaughter it.
- If you found it dead, and it did not eat from it, eat from it.
- If you find your dog with another dog and the dog killed the prey, do not eat it since you did not know which of the two killed it.
- When you shoot an arrow, mention the name of Allāh ﷻ upon shooting.

٦٠٥. وَعَنْ رَافِعِ بْنِ خَدِيجٍ مَرْفُوعًا قَالَ: «ما أَنْهَرَ الدَّمَ، وذُكِرَ اسْمُ اللهِ عَلَيْهِ فَكُلْ، لَيْسَ السِّنُّ والظُّفُرُ، أمّا السِّنُّ: فَعَظْمٌ، وأمّا الظُّفُرُ فَمُدى الحَبَشةِ» مُتَّفَقٌ عَلَيْهِ.

٦٠٦. ويُباحُ صَيْدُ الطلب المعَلَّم بِأنْ يَسْتَرْسِلَ إذا أُرْسِلَ، ويَنْزَجِرَ إذا زُجِرَ، وإذا أمْسَكَ لا يَأْكُلُ ويُسَمِّي صاحِبُها عليها إذا أرسلها.

٦٠٧. وعَنْ عَدِيِّ بْنِ حاتِمٍ قالَ: قالَ رَسُولُ اللهِ ﷺ: «إذا أرْسَلْت كَلْبَكَ المعَلَّم فاذْكُرْ اسْمَ اللهِ عَلَيْهِ،

- فَإِنْ أمسك عليك فأدركته اسم الله عليه،

- وإنْ أدْرَكْتَهُ قَدْ قَتَلَهُ ولَمْ يَأْكُلْ مِنهُ فَكُلْهُ،

- وإنْ وجَدْتَ مَعَ كَلْبِكَ كَلْبًا غَيْرَهُ وقَدْ قَتَلَهُ فَلا تَأْكُلْ، فَإِنَّكَ لا تَدْرِي أيُّهُما قَتَلَهُ؟

- وإنْ رَمَيْتُ سَهْمَكَ فاذْكُرْ اسْمَ اللهِ عَلَيْهِ

- If you find the prey after a day and you find no other mark other than the mark inflicted with your arrow, then eat from it if you wish.
- But if you find that it has drowned in water, then do not eat from it."

608. The Prophet ﷺ said, "Indeed Allāh ﷻ has enjoined proficiency in everything; so, when you kill, do so in an appropriate way, and when you slaughter, do so in an appropriate way. Each one of you should sharpen his knife and allow the slaughtered animal die comfortably." (Muslim)

609. The Prophet ﷺ also said, "Slaughtering the foetus is [achieved by] slaughtering its mother." (Aḥmad)

- فَإِنْ غَابَ عَنْكَ يَوْمًا فَلَمْ تَرَ فِيهِ إِلَّا أَثَرَ سَهْمِكَ فَكُلْ إِنْ شِئْتَ،

- فَإِنْ وجَدْتَهُ غَرِيقًا فِي الماءِ فَلا تَأكل» متفق عليه.

٦٠٨. وفِي الحَدِيثِ: «إِنَّ اللَّهَ كَتَبَ الإِحْسانَ عَلى كل شيءٍ، فَإِذا قَتَلْتُمْ فَأَحْسِنُوا القِتْلَةَ، وإِذا ذَبَحْتُمْ فَأَحْسِنُوا الذِّبْحَةَ، ولْيُحِدَّ أَحدُكُمْ شَفْرَتَهُ، ولْيُرِحْ ذَبِيحَتَهُ» رَواهُ مسلم

٦٠٩. وقال ﷺ: «ذكاة الجنين ذكاة أمه» رواه أحمد

201

# بَابُ الأَيْمان والنُّذُور

# Chapter: Oaths & Vows

610. An oath does not take effect unless it is taken in one of Allāh's ﷻ names or attributes.

611. To swear by other than Allāh ﷻ is *shirk* and thus invalid.

612. The oath that necessitates expiation must be one regarding a future matter.

613. If the oath was regarding a foregone matter - and he lied about the matter whilst knowing the truth - it is considered to be *yamīn ghamūs* (false oath).

614. If he honestly believed a matter that was contrary to the truth, the oath is considered to be *laghwul yamīn* (futile oath), such as saying, "No, by *Allāh*!" or "By *Allāh*!".

615. If one breaks his oath by doing what he swore not to do, or by not doing something he swore to do: it becomes obligatory upon him to expiate for that by:

1. Freeing a slave, or feeding or clothing ten poor people.
2. If one is unable to do that, they should fast three days.

# باب الأيمان والنذور

**٦١٠.** لا تَنْعَقِدُ اليَمِينُ إِلَّا بِاللهِ، أَوِ اسمٍ مِن أَسْمَائِهِ، أَوْ صِفَةٍ مِن صِفَاتِهِ.

**٦١١.** والحَلِفُ بِغَيْرِ اللهِ شِرْكٌ، لا تَنْعَقِدُ بِهِ اليَمِينُ.

**٦١٢.** ولابد أَنْ تَكُونَ اليَمِينُ الموجِبَةُ لِلْكَفَّارَةِ عَلَى أَمْرٍ مُسْتَقْبَلٍ.

**٦١٣.** فَإِنْ كَانَتْ عَلَى ماضٍ وهُوَ كَاذِبٌ عَالِماً فهِي اليَمِين الغَمُوسُ.

**٦١٤.** وإِنْ كَانَ يَظُنُّ صِدْقِ نَفْسِهِ فَهِيَ مِن لَغْوِ اليَمِينِ، كَقَوْلِهِ: لا واللَّهِ، وبَلى واللهِ، في عرض حديثه.

**٦١٥.** وإذا حَنِثَ في يَمِينِهِ بِأَنْ فَعَلَ ما حَلَفَ عَلَى تَرْكِهِ، أَوْ تَرَكَ ما حَلَفَ عَلَى فِعْلِهِ: وجَبَتْ عَلَيْهِ الكَفَّارَةُ:

١. عِتْقُ رَقَبَةٍ، أَوْ إِطْعامُ عَشْرَةِ مَسَاكِينَ، أَوْ كِسْوَتُهُمْ.

٢. فَإِنْ لَمْ يَجِدْ صامَ ثَلاثَةَ أَيَّامٍ.

**616.** ʿAbdur Raḥmān ibn Samurah ﷺ reported that the Prophet ﷺ said, "If you take an oath to do something and later on find another thing better than that, then make expiation for [the dissolution of] your oath and do what is better." (Agreed upon)

**617.** The Prophet ﷺ also said, "Whoever made an oath and then said, "If Allāh ﷻ wills", then there can be no breaking of an oath." (Abū Dāwūd)

**618.** In order to understand the true meaning of the oath, one has to examine:

1. The intention of the one who made the oath.
2. The underlying cause that led to the oath.
3. The part of the oath that indicates the intention of the one who made the oath.

**619.** The exception to the above is in the case on litigation as per the ḥadīth, "The oath is interpreted according to the intention of the one who sought the oath." (Muslim)

٦١٦. وعن عبد الرحمن بن سمرة قال: قال رسول الله ﷺ: «إذا حلفت علي يمين فرأيت غيرها خيرًا منها فكفر عن يَمينك، وائْتِ الذي هو خير» مُتَّفَقٌ عَلَيْهِ.

٦١٧. وِفي الحَدِيثِ: «مَن حَلَفَ عَلى يَمِينٍ، فَقالَ: إنْ شاءَ اللَّهُ، فَلا حِنْثَ عليه» رواه الخمسة

٦١٨. ويُرْجَعُ فِي الأَيْمانِ إلى:

١. نِيَّةُ الحالِفِ.

٢. ثُمَّ إلى السَّبَبِ الذِي هَيَّجَ اليَمِينَ.

٣. ثم إلى اللفظ الدال على النية والإرادة.

٦١٩. إلا في الدعاوي؛ ففي الحديث: «اليمين على نية المستحلف» رَواهُ مُسْلِمٌ

## (Vows)

**620.** Vows are disliked. The Prophet ﷺ prohibited one to make a vow. He ﷺ said, "It does not bring about any good and only comes from a miser." (Agreed upon)

**621.** If one made a vow to do a righteous action it becomes obligatory upon him to do that action as per the statement of the Prophet ﷺ, "Whoever made a vow to obey Allāh ﷻ must obey Allāh ﷻ, and whoever made a vow not to disobey Allāh ﷻ must not disobey Him." (Agreed upon)

**622.** If the vow is regarding a permissible matter, or is similar to making an oath, such as a vow made out of anger or stubbornness, or a vow to perform a sin, then:

- It is not obligatory to fulfil the vow.
- If he does not fulfil the vow, he is to expiate as one who breaks his oath.
- It is prohibited to fulfil a vow that entails committing a sin.

**النُّذُورُ:**

**٦٢٠.** وعَقْدُ النَّذْرِ مَكْرُوهٌ، وقَدْ نَهى النبي ﷺ عن النَّذْرِ، وقالَ: «إنَّهُ لا يَأْتِي بِخَيْرٍ، وإنَّما يُسْتَخْرَجُ بِهِ مِن البَخِيلِ» مُتَّفَقٌ عَلَيْهِ.

**٦٢١.** فإذا عَقَدَهُ عَلى بِرٍّ: وجَبَ عَلَيْهِ الوَفاءُ؛ لِقَوْلِهِ ﷺ: «مَن نَذَرَ أَنْ يُطِيعَ اللهَ فَلْيُطِعْهُ، ومَن نَذَرَ أَنْ يَعْصِيَ اللهَ فَلا يَعْصِهِ» مُتَّفَقٌ عَلَيْهِ

**٦٢٢.** وإنْ كانَ النَّذْرُ مُباحًا أوْ جارِيًا مَجْرى اليَمِينِ كَنَذْرِ اللجاج والغضب أو كان نذر معصية:

- ولم يَجِبْ الوَفاءُ بِهِ.
- وفِيهِ كَفّارَةُ يَمِينٍ إذا لَمْ يُوفِّ بِهِ.
- ويَحْرُمُ الوَفاءُ بِهِ في المعصية.

# بَابُ الجِنَايَات

# The Book of Offences

**623.** Killing without due right is of three types:

1. ʿAmd (intentional killing with enmity). This is when one intends to inflict injury on someone in a manner that would expectedly lead to death.

The guardian of the killed is given the choice of retribution or taking blood money as per the statement of the Prophet ﷺ, "If a relative of anyone is killed, he is entitled to opt for one of two things: either he should be paid blood-money or he can take life [as a just retaliation]." (Agreed upon)

2. Shibh al ʿamd (quasi-intentional killing). This is when one intends to inflict injury on someone in a manner that does not usually lead to death.

3. Khaṭaʾ (accidental). This is when a person unintentionally inflicts an injury on somebody leading to their death, directly or indirectly.

# كِتابُ الجِناياتِ

٦٢٣. القَتْلُ بِغَيْرِ حَقٍّ، يَنْقَسِمُ إلى ثلاثة أقسام:

أحدها: العمد العدوان، وهو: أن يقصده بِجنايَةٍ تَقْتُلُ غالِبًا، فَهذا يُخَيَّرُ الوَلِيُّ فِيهِ بين القتل والديه؛ لِقَوْلِهِ ﷺ: «مَن قُتِلَ له قتيل فهو بخير النظرين: إما أن يقتل، وإما أن يفدى» متفق عليه.

الثّاني: شِبْهِ العَمْدِ، وهُوَ: أَنْ يَتَعَمَّدَ الجِنايَةَ عَلَيْهِ بِما لا يَقْتُلُ غالِبًا.

الثّالِثُ: الخَطَأُ، وهُوَ أَنْ تَقَعَ الجِنايَةُ مِنهُ بِغَيْرِ قَصْدٍ، بمباشرة أو سبب.

209

**624.** In the last case, retribution cannot be applied, rather:

1. An expiation must be taken from the wealth of the killer.

2. His *āqilah* (family), namely his *ʿaṣabah* (close and distant agnate relatives), have the responsibility of paying the blood money. The amount is distributed amongst them according to their circumstances. They are given three years to pay the amount; a third of the amount is to be paid each year.

**625.** The blood money for taking a life and other injuries has been explained in the *ḥadīth* of ʿAmr bin Ḥazm ﷺ, whereby the Prophet ﷺ wrote to the people of Yemen:

"Whoever kills a believer wrongfully and deliberately, is due retaliation unless the relatives of the one killed choose not to opt for that.

- The blood money for a life is one hundred camels.
- The full amount is also due if the following were fully cut off:
    - Nose
    - Tongue
    - Two lips
    - Penis
    - Testicles
    - Backbone (i.e. his back was broken)

٦٢٤. فَفِي الأخير لا قود، بَلْ:

١. الكَفَّارَةُ فِي مالِ القاتِلِ.

٢. والدِّيَةَ عَلَى عاقِلَتِهِ، وهُمْ: عَصِباتُهُ كُلُّهُمْ، قَرِيبِهِمْ وبِعِيدِهِمْ، تَوَزَّعَ عَلَيْهِمْ بِقَدْرِ حالِهِمْ، وتُؤَجَّلُ عَلَيْهِمْ ثَلاثِ سِنِينَ، كُلّ سنةٍ يَحْمِلُونَ ثُلْثُها.

٦٢٥. والدِّياتُ لِلنَّفْسِ وغَيْرِها قَدْ فَصَّلَت فِي حَدِيثِ عَمْرِو بْنِ حَزْمٍ ﷺ: أَنَّ النَّبِيَّ ﷺ إلى أهل اليمن وفيه: أن من اعتبط مؤمنًا قتلاً عن بينة فإنه قَوَدٌ إلّا أنْ يَرْضى أوْلِياءُ المَقْتُولِ.

– وإنْ في النفس: الدية، مائة من الإبل.

– وفِي الأنف إذا أوعب جدعا: الدِّيَةُ.

– وفِي اللِّسانِ: الدِّيَةُ.

– وفِي الشَّفَتَيْنِ: الدِّيَةُ.

– وفِي الذكر: الدية.

– وفِي البيضتين: الدية.

– وفِي الصلب: الدية

211

- Two eyes
- One leg: half the blood money
- A wound in the head: a third of the blood money
- A stabbing that penetrates the body: a third of the blood money
- A head wound which moves a bone: fifteen camels.
- Each finger from the hand or foot: ten camels.
- A tooth: five camels.
- A head wound that exposes the bone: five camels.
- A man may be killed for the retaliation of the killing of a woman.
- Those that have gold should pay one thousand dīnārs." (Abū Dāwūd in *al Marāsīl*)

**626.** Retribution is conditional upon the fulfilment of the following:

1. The killer must be *mukallaf* (legally responsible).

2. The killed must be *ma'ṣūm* (inviolable) and be the same as the perpetrator in terms of faith and freedom. Thus, a Muslim cannot be killed due to [the death of] a disbeliever and a free person cannot be killed due to [the death of] a slave.

3. The killer is not a father of the killed.

- وفي العَيْنَيْنِ: الدِّيَةُ.

- وفي الرِّجْلِ الواحِدَةِ: نِصْفُ الدِّيَةِ.

- وفي المأْمُومَةِ: ثُلُثُ الدِّيَةِ.

- وفي الجائِفَةِ: ثُلُثُ الدِّيَةَ.

- وفي المَنَقِّلَةِ: خَمْسُ عَشْرَةَ مِن الإبل.

- وفي كُلِّ إصْبَعٍ مِن أصابِعِ اليَدِ والرِّجْلِ: عشر من الإبل.

- وفي السنن: خمس مِن الإبِلِ.

- وفي المُوضِحَةِ: خَمْسٌ مِن الإبِلِ.

- وأنَّ الرَّجُلَ يُقْتَلُ بِالمَرْأةِ.

- وعَلى أهْلِ الذَّهَبِ ألف دينار. رواه أبو داود

٦٢٦. ويشترط في وجوب القصاص:

١. كون القاتل مكلفًا.

٢. والمقتول معصومًا، ومكافئًا للجاني في الإسلام، والرق والحرية، فلا يقتل المسلم بالكافر، ولا الحر بالعبد.

٣. وألا يكون والدًا للمقتول، فلا يقتل الأبوان بالولد.

4. There must be an agreement from the guardians of the killed (in wanting retribution).

5. There must be an assurance that there will not be any injustice when fulfilling the retaliation.

**627.** A group of people are to be killed for the death of one person.

**628.** A limb can be taken for a limb if it is possible without any transgression, as per the statement of Allāh ﷻ:

*"In the Torah We prescribed for them a life for a life, an eye for an eye, a nose for a nose, an ear for an ear, a tooth for a tooth, an equal wound for a wound; if anyone forgoes this out of charity, it will serve as atonement for his bad deeds. Those who do not judge according to what God has revealed are doing grave wrong."* (5:45)

**629.** The blood money of a woman is half the blood money of a man, except for an injury that necessitates less than a third of the blood money, in which case it is the same.

٤. ولابد من اتفاقِ الأولياء المكلفين.

٥. والأمن من التعدي في الاستيفاء.

٦٢٧. وتُقْتَل الجَمَاعَةُ بالواحد.

٦٢٨. ويُقادُ كُلُّ عضوٍ بِمِثْلِهِ إذا أمْكَنَ بِدُونِ تعد؛ لِقَوْلِهِ تعالى: ﴿وَكَتَبْنَا عَلَيْهِمْ فِيهَآ أَنَّ ٱلنَّفْسَ بِٱلنَّفْسِ وَٱلْعَيْنَ بِٱلْعَيْنِ وَٱلْأَنفَ بِٱلْأَنفِ وَٱلْأُذُنَ بِٱلْأُذُنِ وَٱلسِّنَّ بِٱلسِّنِّ وَٱلْجُرُوحَ قِصَاصٌ فَمَن تَصَدَّقَ بِهِۦ فَهُوَ كَفَّارَةٌ لَّهُۥ وَمَن لَّمْ يَحْكُم بِمَآ أَنزَلَ ٱللَّهُ فَأُوْلَٰئِكَ هُمُ ٱلظَّٰلِمُونَ ۝﴾ [المائدة: ٤٥]

٦٢٩. ودِيَةُ المرأةِ عَلى نِصْفِ دِيَةِ الذَّكَر، إلّا فِيما دُونَ ثُلُثِ الدِّيَةَ فَهُما سَواءٌ.

# كِتَابُ الحُدُود

# The Book of Prescribed Punishments

**630.** A prescribed punishment (*ḥadd*) cannot be applied except upon the legally responsible (*mukallaf*) who is aware of the unlawfulness of the crime.

**631.** It is not commissioned except by the head of state or his deputy, with exception to the *sayyid* (slave owner), as he has the sole right to flog his slave.

**632.** The flogging of a slave should be half the amount of a free person.

### The Punishment for Fornication/Adultery

**633.** The punishment for fornication/adultery - which is to have sexual intercourse, whether vaginal or anal - is as follows:

- A *muḥṣan* i.e. a person who had married and consummated the marriage whilst they were both free and legally liable, is to be stoned to death.
- A non-*muhsan* is to be flogged one hundred times and exiled from their homeland for one year.

# كتاب الحدود

**٦٣٠.** لا حد إلا على مُكَلَّفٍ مُلْتَزِمٍ عالِمٍ بِالتَّحْرِيمِ.

**٦٣١.** ولا يُقِيمُهُ إلَّا الإمامُ أوْ نائِبُهُ، إلَّا السَّيِّدُ، فَإنَّ لَهُ إقامَتُهُ بِالجَلْدِ خاصَّةً عَلى رَقِيقِهِ.

**٦٣٢.** وحَدُّ الرقيق في الجلد: نصف حد الحر.

## حد الزنا

**٦٣٣.** فحد الزِّنا وهُوَ فِعْلُ الفاحِشَةِ في قُبُلٍ أوْ دُبُرٍ:

- إنْ كانَ مُحْصَنًا–وهُوَ الذِي قَدْ تَزَوَّجَ ووَطِئَها وهُما حُرّانِ مُكَلَّفانِ–فَهَذا يُرْجَمُ حَتّى يَمُوتَ.

- وإنْ كانَ غَيْرَ مُحْصِنٍ: جُلِدَ مائة جلدة، وغُرِّبَ عن وطنه عامًا.

**634.** The above is only applied on the condition that the *zānī* admits to it four times, or four just witnesses testify that they clearly saw the act.

Allāh ﷻ says:

*"Strike the female fornicator and the male fornicator one hundred times. Do not let compassion for them keep you from carrying out God's law - if you believe in God and the Last Day - and ensure that a group of believers witnesses the punishment."* (24:2)

ʿUbādah Ibn al Ṣāmiṭ reported in a *marfūʿ ḥadīth*, "Take from me, take from me! Allāh ﷻ has ordained a way for those [women]. When an unmarried male commits fornication with an unmarried female, [they should receive]) one hundred lashes and be banished for one year. And in case of a married male committing adultery with a married female, they shall receive one hundred lashes and be stoned to death." (Muslim)

Stoning the adulterer alone was the final method of punishment, as was the case with Māʿiz and al-Ghāmidiyyah.

٦٣٤. ولَكِنْ بِشَرْطِ أَنْ يُقِرَّ بِهِ أَرْبَعَ مَرّاتٍ، أَوْ يَشْهَدَ عَلَيْهِ أَرْبَعَةُ عُدُولٍ يُصَرِّحُونَ بِشَهادَتِهِمْ.

قال تعالى: ﴿ٱلزَّانِيَةُ وَٱلزَّانِي فَٱجْلِدُواْ كُلَّ وَٰحِدٍ مِّنْهُمَا مِاْئَةَ جَلْدَةٍۖ﴾ [النور: ٢]

وعن عبادة بن الصامت مرفوعًا: «خذوا عني، خذوا عني، فقد جعل الله لهن سبيلًا: البكر جلد مائة ونفي سنة، والثيب بالثيب: جلد مائة والرجم» رَواهُ مُسْلِمٌ.

وآخِرُ الأَمْرَيْنِ الِاقْتِصارُ عَلَى رَجْمِ المُحصن، كما في قصة ماعز والغامدية

## The Punishment for *Qadhf* (Accusing a Person of Adultery Without Proof)

**635.** Whoever accuses a *muḥṣan* of committing adultery, or testifies to it without there being the sufficient number of witnesses, is to be flogged eighty times.

**636.** Accusing a non-*muḥṣan* of committing fornication entails *taʿzīr* (discretionary punishment).

**637.** A *Muḥṣan* is a free, mature, sane, and chaste Muslim.

## *Taʿzīr:* Discretionary Punishment

**638.** It is obligatory for *taʿzīr* to be carried out for every sin that neither entails a prescribed punishment nor an expiation.

## حد القَذْف

٦٣٥. ومن قذف بالزني مُحْصَنًا، أَوْ شَهِدَ عَلَيْهِ بِهِ، ولَمْ تَكْمُلْ الشهادة: جلد ثمانين جلدة.

٦٣٦. وقذف غير المحصن فيه التعزيز.

٦٣٧. والمحصن: هو الحر البالغ المسلم العاقل العفيف.


## التعزيز

٦٣٨. والتعزيز واجِبٌ فِي كُلِّ مَعْصِيَةٍ لا حَدَّ فِيها ولا كفارة

## The Prescribed Punishment for Theft

**639.** Whoever steals a quarter of a *dīnār* or more of gold or something worth an equivalent amount from a secure place is to have his hand amputated from his wrist and then have it cauterised with hot oil.

**640.** If he steals for a second time, his left foot should be amputated from the ankle and then have it cauterised with hot oil.

**641.** If he steals again, he should be imprisoned.

**642.** Anything other than the hand and foot should not be amputated.

Allāh ﷻ says:

*"Cut off the hands of thieves, whether they are man or woman, as punishment for what they have done - a deterrent from God: God is almighty and wise."* (5:38)

ʿAʾishah ﷺ reported in a *marfūʿ ḥadīth*, "The hand of a thief should not be amputated except for a quarter of a *dīnār* or more." (Agreed upon)

**643.** The Prophet ﷺ said, "The hand is not to be amputated for taking fruit or the pith of a palm tree." (Abū Dāwūd)

## حد السرقة

**٦٣٩.** ومن سرق رُبْعَ دِينارٍ مِن الذَّهَبِ أوْ ما يُساوِيهِ مِنَ المالِ مِن حِرْزِهِ: قُطِعَتْ يَدُهُ اليُمْنى من مفصِل الكف، وحُسِمَتْ.

**٦٤٠.** فإنْ عادَ قُطِعَتْ رِجْلُهُ اليُسْرى مِن مَفْصِلِ الكعب وحُسِمَتْ.

**٦٤١.** فإن عاد حُبِسَ.

**٦٤٢.** ولا يقطع غير يدٍ ورجل.

قال تعالى: ﴿وَٱلسَّارِقُ وَٱلسَّارِقَةُ فَٱقْطَعُوٓا۟ أَيْدِيَهُمَا جَزَآءًۢ بِمَا كَسَبَا نَكَٰلًا مِّنَ ٱللَّهِ ۗ وَٱللَّهُ عَزِيزٌ حَكِيمٌ﴾ [المائدة:٣٨]

وعن عائشة رضي الله عنهامرفوعًا: «لا تقطع يد سارِقٍ إلا في ربع دينار فصاعدًا» مُتَّفَقٌ عَلَيْهِ.

**٦٤٣.** وِفي الحَدِيثِ: «لا قَطْعَ فِي ثمرٍ ولا كَثَر» رواه أهل السنن

223

### The punishment for ḥirābah (banditry)

**644.** Allāh ﷻ says regarding bandits:

*"Those who wage war against God and His Messenger and strive to spread corruption in the land should be punished by death, crucifixion, the amputation of an alternate hand and foot, or banishment from the land: a disgrace for them in this world, and then a terrible punishment in the Hereafter"* (5:33)

**645.** Bandits are those who attack people on the roads and rob them by plundering or killing them.

1. Whoever kills and takes someone's wealth is to be killed and crucified.
2. Whoever kills another person must be killed.
3. Whoever takes someone's wealth should have his right hand and left foot amputated.
4. Whoever frightens people should be exiled.

### Rebellion

**646.** Whoever rebels against the ruler intending to remove him is considered to be a *bāghī* (rebel).

## حد الحرابة

٦٤٤. وقالَ تَعالى في المحاربِينَ: ﴿إِنَّمَا جَزَٰٓؤُاْ ٱلَّذِينَ يُحَارِبُونَ ٱللَّهَ وَرَسُولَهُۥ وَيَسۡعَوۡنَ فِي ٱلۡأَرۡضِ فَسَادًا أَن يُقَتَّلُوٓاْ أَوۡ يُصَلَّبُوٓاْ أَوۡ تُقَطَّعَ أَيۡدِيهِمۡ وَأَرۡجُلُهُم مِّنۡ خِلَٰفٍ أَوۡ يُنفَوۡاْ مِنَ ٱلۡأَرۡضِۚ ذَٰلِكَ لَهُمۡ خِزۡيٞ فِي ٱلدُّنۡيَاۖ وَلَهُمۡ فِي ٱلۡأٓخِرَةِ عَذَابٌ عَظِيمٌ﴾

[المائدة:٣٣]

٦٤٥. وهُمُ الذِينَ يَخْرُجُونَ عَلى النّاسِ، ويَقْطَعُونَ الطَّرِيقَ عَلَيْهِمْ بِنَهْبٍ أو قَتْلٍ.

١. فَمَن قتل وأخذ مالاً: قُتِلَ وصُلِبَ،

٢. ومَن قَتَلَ: تَحَتَّمَ قَتْلُهُ،

٣. ومَن أخَذَ مالًا: قُطِعَتْ يَدُهُ اليُمْنى ورِجْلُهُ اليُسْرى،

٤. ومَن أخافَ النّاسَ: نُفِيَ من الأرض.


## البُغاةِ

٦٤٦. ومَن خَرَجَ عَلى الإمامِ يُرِيدُ إزالَتَهُ عَنْ مَنصِبِهِ: فَهُوَ باغٍ.

**647.** The ruler should communicate with them and bring an end to anything unlawful under his authority that they have against him. He should also try and remove any misunderstandings they may have.

**648.** If they stop their mischief, he should leave them alone, otherwise he should fight against them if they choose rebellion by force.

**649.** It is upon his subjects to assist him in fighting them.

**650.** If one is compelled to kill them or destroy their wealth, there is nothing upon the defendant (in terms of compensation).

**651.** If the defendant is killed, he is considered to be a martyr.

**652.** Those of them that flee should not be followed, and their wounded should not be killed. Their wealth is not war booty and hence not permissible to take. Likewise, their offspring are not taken as captives.

**653.** No compensation is due from the two factions for lives that are lost or wealth that is destroyed during the fighting.

٦٤٧. وعَلى الإمامِ: مُراسَلَةُ البُغاة، وإزالة ما ينقمون عليه

٦٤٩. وعَلى رَعيَّتِهِ: مَعُونَتُهُ عَلى قِتالِهِمْ.

٦٥٠. فَإِنْ اضطر إلى قتلهم أو تلف مالهم: فلا شيء عَلى الدّافِعِ.

٦٥١. وإنْ قُتِلَ الدّافِعُ كانَ شَهيدًا.

٦٥٢. ولا يُتَّبَعُ لَهُمْ مُدْبِرٌ، ولا يُجْهَزُ عَلى جَريحٍ، ولا يُغْنَمُ لَهُمْ مالٌ، ولا يُسْبى لَهُمْ ذُرِّيَّةٌ.

٦٥٣. ولا ضَمانَ عَلى أَحَدِ الفَريقَيْنِ فيما أُتْلِفَ حالَ الحَرْبِ مِن نفوسٍ وأمْوالٍ.

# باب حُكْمُ المُرْتَدِّ

# Chapter: Apostasy

**654.** An apostate is one who leaves the fold of *Islām* through an action, statement, belief, or doubt.

**655.** The scholars have mentioned the details of that which takes one out of the fold of *Islām*. These matters either entail denying what the Prophet ﷺ was sent with in totality or partially, as long as he is not *mutaʾawwil* (someone who offers a divergent interpretation of a text) when rejecting a text.

**656.** An apostate is given three days to repent. If he does not return to *Islām* he is to be killed by the sword.

# باب حُكْمُ المُرْتَدّ

٦٥٤. والمرْتَدُّ هُوَ: مَن خَرَجَ عَنْ دِينِ الإِسْلامِ إلى الكُفْرِ، بفعلٍ أوْ قولٍ أوْ اعتقادٍ أوْ شَكٍّ.

٦٥٥. وقَدْ ذَكَرَ العُلَماءُ رَحِمَهُمُ اللَّهُ تَفاصِيلَ ما يَخْرُجُ بِهِ العَبْدُ مِنَ الإِسْلامِ، وتَرْجِعُ كُلُّها إلى جَحْدِ ما جاء به الرسولُ ﷺ، أوْ جَحْدِ بَعْضِهِ غَيْرَ مُتَأَوِّلٍ في جَحْدِ البَعْضِ.

٦٥٦. فَمَنِ ارْتَدَّ: أُسْتُتِيبَ ثَلاثَةَ أَيَّامٍ، فَإِنْ رجع وإلا قتل بالسيف.

# كِتَابُ القَضَاء والدَعَاوى والبَيِّنَات وأَنْوَاع الشَّهَادَات

# The Book of Judicial Rulings, Claims, Evidence & Types of Testimonies

**657.** Passing judicial rulings are indispensable for people and is therefore considered a communal obligation.

**658.** It is obligatory upon the ruler to appoint a sufficient number of people who can oversee this obligation. Such individuals must have knowledge of judging according to Islamic Law and knowledge of how to apply such laws upon people's respective circumstances.

**659.** The ruler must appoint the most appropriate person for such a position and then the most appropriate thereafter, taking into consideration the required qualities for a judge.

**660.** It becomes an individual obligation to take such a position if he is qualified and there is nobody else to take that position, as long as it does not preoccupy him from something more important.

**661.** The Prophet ﷺ said, "The onus of proof is upon the claimant, and the taking of an oath is to be said by the one who denies." (Tirmidhī)

# كِتابُ القَضاءِ والدَّعاوى، والبَيِّناتِ وأنْواعِ الشَّهاداتِ

٦٥٧. والقَضاءُ لابد لِلنَّاسِ مِنهُ، فَهُوَ فَرْضُ كِفايَةٍ.

٦٥٨. يَجِبُ عَلى الإمامِ نَصْبُ مَن يَحْصُلُ فيهِ الكِفايَةُ مِمَّنْ لَهُ مَعْرِفَةٌ بِالقَضاءِ بِمَعْرِفَةِ الأحْكامِ الشَّرْعِيَّةِ، وتَطْبيقِها عَلى الوَقائِعِ الجارِيَةِ بَيْنَ النَّاسِ.

٦٥٩. وعَلَيهِ أنْ يُوَلِّيَ الأمْثَلَ فالأمْثَلَ فِي الصِّفاتِ المُعْتَبَرَةِ فِي القاضِي.

٦٦٠. ويَتَعَيَّنُ عَلى مَن كانَ أهْلًا، ولَمْ يُوجَدْ غَيْرُهُ، ولَمْ يَشْغَلْهُ عَمّا هُوَ أهُمْ مِنهُ.

٦٦١. وقَدْ قالَ النَّبِيُّ ﷺ: «البَيِّنَةُ عَلى المدَّعِي، واليَمِينُ عَلى مَن أنْكَرَ.»

662. The Prophet ﷺ said, "I judge according to what I hear." (Agreed upon)

663. If someone makes claim to property, it is upon him to produce evidence, which is in the form of bringing:

1. Two just male witnesses, or
2. One man and two women, or
3. One man accompanied with an oath from the claimant.

As per the saying of Allāh ﷻ:

*"Call in two men as witnesses. If two men are not there, then call one man and two women out of those you approve as witnesses..."*(2:282)

The Prophet ﷺ passed a judgment taking as evidence a witness and an oath. This is based upon an authentic *ḥadīth*.

664. If the claimant did not have a *bayyinah* (proof), the defendant has to swear an oath and will therefore be deemed innocent.

٦٦٢. وقال: «إنما أَقْضِي بِنَحْوِ مَا أَسْمع»

٦٦٣. فمن ادَّعى مالًا ونَحْوَهُ فَعَلَيْهِ البَيّنةُ:

١. إمّا شاهِدانِ عَدْلانِ،

٢. أوْ رَجُلٌ وامْرَأتانِ،

٣. أوْ رَجُلٌ ويَمينُ المدَّعي؛ لِقَوْلِهِ تَعالى: ﴿وَٱسْتَشْهِدُواْ شَهِيدَيْنِ مِن رِّجَالِكُمْ فَإِن لَّمْ يَكُونَا رَجُلَيْنِ فَرَجُلٌ وَٱمْرَأَتَانِ مِمَّن تَرْضَوْنَ مِنَ ٱلشُّهَدَآءِ﴾ [البَقَرَة: ٢٨٢]

«وقَدْ قَضى النَّبِيُّ ﷺ بالشاهد مع اليمين» وهو حديث صحيح.

٦٦٤. فإن لم يكن له بينة: حلف المدَّعى عَلَيْهِ وبَرِئَ

233

**665.** However, if he refuses to take an oath, he will be judged as refusing to testify in court or the claimant will be asked to swear an oath again. Thus, if he (i.e. the claimant) swears an oath with the defendant refusing to give an oath, the claimant will win the case.

**666.** A type of *bayyinah* is: a proof that is indicative of either litigants' truthfulness:

1. For example, if the property is in the possession of one of the litigants, it will be his if he swears an oath.
2. Another example is if two people claim the right to an asset that can only belong to one of them, such as disputing with a carpenter over one of his tools, or a with a blacksmith over one of his tools, and so on.

**667.** It is a communal obligation to bear witness of a person's right.

**668.** It is an individual obligation to give testimony if requested.

**669.** It is a condition that the witness is just, both outwardly and inwardly.

**670.** The just person is one whom people accept and are pleased with as per the saying of Allāh ﷻ, "*...from those who you accept as witnesses*" (2:282)

٦٦٥. فَإِنَّ نَكَلَ عَنِ الحَلِفِ قُضِيَ عَلَيْهِ بِالنُّكُولِ، أَوْ رُدَّتِ اليَمِينُ عَلَى المُدَّعِي، فَإِذَا حَلَفَ مَعَ نُكُولِ المُدَّعى عَلَيْهِ أَخَذَ ما اِدَّعى بِهِ.

٦٦٦. ومِنَ البَيِّنَةِ: القَرِينَةُ الدَّالَّةُ عَلَى صِدْقِ أَحَدِ المُتَداعِيَيْنِ:

١. مِثْلُ أَنْ تَكُونَ العَيْنُ المُدَّعى بِها بِيَدِ أَحَدِهِما، فَهِيَ لَهُ بِيَمِينِهِ.

٢. ومِثْلُ أَنْ يَتَداعى اثنانِ مالًا لا يصلح إلا لأحداهما، كَتَنازُعِ نَجَّارٍ ونَحْوِهِ٤ بِآلَةِ نِجارَتِهِ، وحدادٍ ونَحْوِهِ بآلة حدادةٍ، ونَحو ذلك.

٦٦٧. وتَحَمُّلُ الشهادة في حقوق الآدميين: فرض كفاية.

٦٦٨. وأداؤها: فرض عين.

٦٦٩. ويشترط أن يكون الشاهد عدلا ظاهرا وباطنا.

٦٧٠. والعدل: هو من رضيه الناس لقوله تعالى: ﴿مِمَّنْ تَرْضَوْنَ مِنَ الشُّهَداءِ﴾ [البقرة: ٢٨٢]

**671.** It is not permitted for the witness to testify to something unless he has knowledge of it by either:

1. Seeing it
2. Hearing it from the accused
3. The matter becoming so well known in matters that require it, such as lineage or the like.

The Prophet ﷺ said to a man, "Do you see the sun?" To which he replied, 'Yes'. The Prophet ﷺ then said, "Then testify in a case as clear as the sun, otherwise, leave the matter." (Reported by Ibn 'Udayy)

**672.** Impediments to the acceptance of a testimony include: suspicion of untruthfulness, such as one's parents testifying for them or vice versa, or a spouse testifying for their spouse, or a person testifying against his enemy.

The Prophet ﷺ said, "The testimony of a deceitful man and woman, or one who harbours rancour against his brother, and the testimony of one who is dependent on a family, are all not allowed." (Abū Dāwūd)

**673.** The Prophet ﷺ also said, "Whoever takes a false oath to deprive somebody of his property will meet Allāh ﷻ in a state where He will be angry with him." (Agreed upon)

٦٧١. ولا يجوز أن يشهد إلا بما يعلمه:

١. برؤية،

٢ –أو سماع من المشهود عليه،

٣ –أو استفاضة يحصل بها العلم في الأشياء التي يُحتاج فيها إليها، كالأنساب ونحوها.

وقال النبي ﷺ لرجل: «ترى الشمس»؟ قال: نعم، قال: «على مثلها فاشهد أو دع» رواه ابن عدي.

٦٧٢. ومن موانع الشهادة: مَظِنَّةُ التهمة، كشهادة الوالدين لأولادهم، وبالعكس، وأحد الزوجين للآخر، والعدو على عدوه،

كما في الحديث: «لا تجوز شهادة خائن ولا خائنة، ولا ذي غمر على أخيه، ولا تجوز شهادة القانع لأهل البيت.» رواه أحمد وأبو داود

٦٧٣. وفي الحديث: «من حلف على يمين يقتطع بها مال امرئ مسلم هو فيها فاجر: لقي الله وهو عليه غضبان» متفق عليه

# بَابُ القِسْمَة

# Chapter: Division

**674.** *Qismah* (division of jointly owned property) is of two types:

1. Enforced division: this is a type of division that entails no harm nor requires any compensation, such as things of exact equivalence, spacious property, or large areas of land.

2. Mutually consensual division: this harms one of the partners when dividing or requires compensation. Here, there must be mutual consent amongst all partners.

If one of the partners requests that his share be sold, it must be sold.

If they decide to lease the property, the rent is divided amongst them according to how much each partner owns.

And Allāh ﷻ knows best.

# بابُ القِسْمَةِ

٦٧٤. وهِيَ نَوْعانِ:

١. قِسْمَةُ إِجْبارٍ، فيما لا ضَرَرَ فيهِ، ولا رَدَّ عِوَضٍ، كالمِثْلِياتِ، والدور الكبار، والأملاك الواسعة.

٢. وقِسْمَةُ تراضٍ، وهِيَ ما فيهِ ضَرَرٌ عَلى أحَدِ الشُّرَكاءِ في القِسْمَةِ، أوْ فيهِ رَدُّ عوضٍ، فلابد فيها مِن رِضا الشُّرَكاءِ كُلِّهِمْ.

وإنْ طَلَبَ أحَدُهُمْ فيها البَيْعَ: وجَبَتْ إجابَتُهُ، وإنْ أجَّرُوها: كانَتْ الأُجْرَةُ فيها عَلى قَدْرِ مَلِكِهِمْ فيها.

والله أعلم.

# بَابُ الإِقْرَار

# Chapter: Confession

**675.** *Iqrār* is a person's confession of a right upon him by using any word indicative of confession, on the condition that the confessor is legally responsible.

**676.** It is amongst the most effective forms of evidence.

**677.** It covers all areas of knowledge, such as: worship, contracts, marriage, offences, and so on.

**678.** A *ḥadīth* states, "There is no excuse for the one that has confessed."

**679.** It is obligatory upon a person to confess all rights he owes to others in order to absolve himself from any liability by either fulfilling the rights or being forgiven.

May the peace and blessings of Allāh ﷻ be upon our Master and Prophet Muhammad ﷺ, his family, and companions.

Written by the poor servant to his Lord, hoping that his Lord rectifies his religious and worldly affairs, ʿAbd al Raḥmān Ibn Nāṣir Ibn Saʿdī. May Allāh ﷻ forgive him, his parents, and all Muslims.

# باب الإقرار

٦٧٥. وهو اعترف الإنْسانِ بِحَقٍّ عَلَيْهِ، بِكُلِّ لَفْظٍ دالٍّ عَلى الإقْرارِ، بِشَرْطِ كَوْنِ المقِرِّ مُكَلَّفًا.

٦٧٦. وهُوَ مِن أَبْلَغِ البَيِّناتِ.

٦٧٧. ويَدْخُلُ في جَميعِ أبْوابِ العِلْمِ مِن العِباداتِ والمعامَلاتِ والأنْكِحَةِ والجِناياتِ وغَيْرِها.

٦٧٨. وفي الحَديثِ: «لا عُذْرَ لِمَن أقَرَّ».

٦٧٩. ويَجِبُ عَلى الإنْسانِ: أنْ يَعْتَرِفَ بِجَميعِ الحُقُوقِ التي عَلَيْهِ لِلْآدَمِيِّينَ لِيَخْرُجَ مِنَ التَّبِعَةِ بِأداءٍ أوْ اِسْتِحْلالٍ. والله أعلم.

وصَلَّى اللَّهُ عَلى سَيِّدِنا ونَبِيِّنا مُحَمَّدٍ وعَلى آلهِ وأصحابه وسلم تسليمًا كثيراً.

عَلَّقَهُ كاتِبُهُ الفَقيرُ إلى اللهِ، الرَّاجِي مِنهُ أنْ يُصْلِحَ دِينَهُ ودُنْياهُ: عَبْدُ الرَّحْمَنِ بْنُ ناصِرِ بْنِ سَعْدِيٍّ، غَفَرَ اللَّهُ لَهُ ولِوالِدَيْهِ ولِجَميعِ المسْلِمينَ،

(Copied from the original manuscript on the 3<sup>rd</sup> of *Dhul Ḥijjah* 1359h, (1/1/1941.ad) and all praise is due to Allāh , who, by His blessings are righteous actions completed.)

نَقَلْتهُ مِنَ الأصْلِ، وتَمَّ النَّقْلُ ٣/ ذو الحجة/ ١٣٥٩،
والحمد لله الذي بنعمته تتم الصالحات.

# Bibliography

قائمة المراجع

Al Saʿdī, ʿAbd al Raḥmān bin Nāṣir. *Manhaj al Sālikīn*. Riyāḍ: Dār ibn al Jawzi, 2003.

Al Jibrīn, ʿAbd Allāh bin ʿAbd al Raḥmān. *Ibhāj al Muʾminīn bi-Sharḥ Manhaj al Sālikīn*. Riyāḍ: Madār al Waṭan, 2001.

Qalʿajī, Muḥammad Rawwās. *Muʿjam Lughah al Fuqahāʾ*. Beirut: Dār al Nafāʾis, 1996.